ANGELS AND DEMONS

ANGELS AND DEMONS

By

Mrs. George C. Needham

MOODY PRESS
CHICAGO

CONTENTS

CONTENTS

INTRODUCTION

THE READER will find in this book a timely discussion of a most important subject. It is a theme about which most professing Christians are deplorably ignorant, although it profoundly affects both their peace and safety along the journey of life. They do not know that angels and demons are attending their steps—the former to minister to their need, the latter to murder them, body and soul, if permitted to have their malignant way.

Indeed, many who claim to believe the Bible, receive with a smile of incredulity any allusion, in public or private discourse, to these supernatural beings. At a recent dinner party, the hostess, who is prominent in an evangelical church, asked a gentleman if he accepted as true the doctrine of a personal Devil. "I most certainly do," was the reply, "since I accept the sacred Scriptures as a revelation from God." She laughed at the thought that anyone of ordinary culture could retain a superstition, which in her judgment belonged to the Dark Ages.

7

This lady no doubt represents a vast number in all the churches, who do not read the Bible, or who do not hear it faithfully preached, or who do not care to breast the current of modern infidel thought that is carrying Christendom farther and farther from God. In one respect at least they stand where a large and influential sect stood years ago, nor has there been the slightest advance, notwithstanding the boasted progress of the nineteenth century. "The Sadducees say that there is no resurrection, neither angel, nor spirit" (Acts 23:8); and so say today multitudes, who would be shocked if told that they do not receive the teachings of the inspired Book.

For the existence of a personal Devil, and of angels and demons, who are constantly concerned in human affairs, we have precisely the same evidence that convinces us of the birth, the life, the death, and the resurrection of our Lord Jesus Christ. The Word of God is not more explicit in its testimony upon the one truth than it is upon the other; nor in the nature of the case is it a question that is to be determined by the intellect, or rather, by the ignorance of man. The existence of angels and demons, or their immediate but invisible relation to man, is not a whit more impossible or inconceivable, even according to reason, than the incarnation of the eternal God in the form of a little babe, and the triumphant ascension of His mangled body from the tomb. He who denies either is blinded by "the god of this world."

Mrs. Needham, therefore, has rendered admirable and acceptable service in calling attention to a solemn truth so little known, or so little heeded. In a style singularly lucid, with a loyalty to Scripture that commands respect, and with great force of exposition, argument, and illustration, she has shown that angels and demons are hovering near the children of God on their march to the judgment seat of Christ. Her book ought to be widely read, and thoughtfully pondered by earnest souls, for it is highly instructive and intensely interesting. May the Master speed it on its way to honor His ever-living Word, and to hasten His glorious coming!
—REV. JAMES H. BROOKES, D. D.

1

EXISTENCE OF ANGELS

MANKIND HAS ALWAYS BELIEVED in unseen creatures peopling the aerial spaces. The Bible sustains this idea, informing us that these spiritual intelligences do exist, and in close proximity to our world; that they are divided into two vast hosts: the one active in good ministries for our race; the other intent on annoying and injuring us; the one host designated as angels, loyal to God; the other called demons, apostates under Satan and rebels against God. To investigate what the Scriptures reveal concerning these unseen beings is the object of this book.

The earthward ministry of angels is a prime fact of Scripture, quite as distinctly stated as is the ministry of the Holy Spirit. Nor is it recorded only as a past fact that in earlier dispensations prior to the incarnation angels were frequent visitors to our world as messengers of God to governments and to individuals. Very majestic and deeply wonderful are the inspired words teaching us that even now the angels are "all ministering spirits, sent forth to minister for them who shall be heirs of salvation" (Heb. 1:14).

Yet, strangely enough, only slight prominence is accorded to this marvelous truth in modern Christian teaching. Hence, as is the case with regard to other doctrines, those which are dimly apprehended by the mind are feebly appreciated by the heart. Neglecting to study the ministry of angels, the church of God has become impoverished in her experiences of divine providences, and destitute of that succor and comfort which it is her appointed office to supply.

Possibly the present prosperity of the church may furnish a partial explanation of her indifference to the guardianship of angels. Carnal security does certainly characterize her in this age. She has been saying—and in one sense, truthfully—"I am rich and increased with goods, and have need of nothing." The fires of martyrdom were burned out long ago. The instruments of torture are rusty and dull of edge. The enemies of the cross have made a covenant with the followers of the Lamb. Even Satan employs his arts in covering his naked hideousness, and transforms himself under celestial garb to work wickedness.

"Where is the necessity of angelic ministry?" asks this self-confident and comfortable church of God. The perils of Egypt and the pilgrimage of Israel pertain not to us. No autocratic monarch menaces our

Christian liberty by fiery furnace or savage beast. No Syrian hosts encompass us around. We "are at ease in Zion," and "Jerusalem is a quiet habitation." Thus has the church been a long time vaunting itself, while the angels of God, unrecognized and undesired, appear to have refrained their precious offices, and withheld their visitations, even as of old they once left Jacob to his carnal plans and fleshly fears.

But the flock of God shall not always continue in this apathy of security. Our Lord's own prophetic words warrant us in expecting days of exceeding peril at the close of this dispensation. Already the first premonitory throes are upon us. Trials, so fierce that unassisted flesh and blood may not withstand them, are announced to come upon the world, casting reflex influence upon the followers of Christ. It was before Noah entered the ark that carnal indifference, unbelief, and mockery surrounded him. It was before Lot was snatched out of Sodom that the unclean conduct of the wicked vexed his righteous soul for many days. The conclusion is self-evident, for our Lord himself has established the parallel.

Whether or not that which is technically designated the Great Tribulation shall be precipitated before the Church is gathered unto the Lord by translation, we may not here turn aside to discuss. It is certainly taught that some measure of special sorrows shall afflict those living near the extremity of this age. And in that coming period, which many moral signs indicate to be not far distant, the presence and help of angels upon earth shall be greatly needed by the harassed and imperiled company of the elect. Then, certainly if not now, the teaching concerning the ministry of these celestial servants will be recognized and welcomed as "meat in due season" to the household of God.

We presume it will be conceded by all, that, in whatever way the Lord God has been pleased to communicate His truth to man, the divine agency in these revelations has been the Holy Spirit. We proceed, then, to state two remarkable Scripture facts, which reveal something very peculiar in the ministry of angels.

1. The Holy Spirit, under whatever dispensation He has operated, has designedly limited Himself to the truth of God, thus becoming the divine Interpreter to impart information concerning spiritual matters exclusively.

2. To the angel, or angels, as converse to this, has been committed the administration of affairs material to sense. Thus, when Hagar was fainting in the wilderness, the angel showed her a fountain. When Joshua was in a strait, the angle appeared as the Lord's captain with a sword. When Peter was in prison, an angel drew back the iron bolts and talked with the apostle about such material things as his girdle, cloak, and sandals.

The united manifestation of this double principle in connection with single individuals is very striking. The angel of the Lord appeared to Gideon, making a sign out of the kid, cakes, and broth, which he had prepared. But it was the Spirit of the Lord that followed, who qualified Gideon for his work. Four times in the history of the judges, this double, united ministry is traceable. But most remarkable was it in the life of our Lord. He was led of the Spirit, and taught of the Spirit, and filled with the Spirit. But He was fed by angels, defended by angels, and strengthened by angels. The same distinction prevailed in connection with the revelation of the law and Gospel. The law, affirmed to have been spoken by angels, was engraved on material tables of stone (Acts 7:53; Gal. 3:19; Heb. 2:2). The Gospel, which was ministered of the Spirit, was written upon fleshy tables of the heart (II Cor. 3:3).

Thus, angels are associated with the more tangible phase of heavenly service, while the Holy Spirit applies Himself to the ministry of the inward and unseen.

The term *angel* designates an office, rather than describes a person. In itself, unqualified by circumstances, it simply means "a messenger." An angel might be any of the "sons of God"—heavenly, as for instance, the seraphim; or earthly, like human prophets. Thus we understand how, in Malachi, Jesus is called, "The angel [i. e., the Messenger] of the covenant" (Mal. 3:1); since in Hebrews it is declared that He never took on Him the nature of angels (Heb. 1:5, 6; 2:16).

The word *angel* is employed in seven senses in Scripture:

1. For human messengers.

"And David sent messengers unto the men of Jabesh-gilead, and said unto them, Blessed be ye of the Lord, that ye have showed this kindness unto your lord, even unto Saul, and have buried him" (II Sam. 2:5).

"And when the messengers of John were departed, he began to speak unto the people concerning John, What went ye out into the wilderness for to see? A reed shaken with the wind?" (Luke 7:24).

2. For human messengers bearing a divine message.

"Then spake Haggai the Lord's messenger in the Lord's message unto the people, saying, I am with you, saith the Lord" (Hag. 1:13).

"And my temptation which was in my flesh ye despised not, nor rejected; but received me as an angel of God, even as Christ Jesus" (Gal. 4:14).

3. For impersonal providences.

"And lest I should be exalted above measure through the abundance of the revelations, there was given to me a thorn in the flesh, the messenger of Satan to buffet me, lest I should be exalted above measure" (II Cor. 12:7).

4. For bishops or pastors.

"Unto the angel of the church of Ephesus write .... Unto the angel of the church of the Laodiceans write" (Rev. 2:1; 3:14).

5. For demons without bodies, who roam the air in partial bondage and take possession of men.

These are called the Devil's angels, he being stated to be their prince (Matt. 12:24; 25:41).

6. For heavenly beings, such as guarded Jacob. "Jacob went on his way, and the angels of God met him. And when Jacob saw them, he said, This is God's host; and he called the name of that place Mahanaim" (Gen. 32:1, 2).

7. For one of pre-eminent excellency, named distinctively The angel of the Lord (Exod. 3:2).

The English version being uniformly discriminating, there is no difficulty in distinguishing in nearly every instance between the heavenly angel and the human messenger.

2

THE NATURE OF ANGELS

I T CAN BE ABUNDANTLY PROVED that angels are actual beings and not impersonal influences. They ate with Abraham, and took hold of Lot by the hand. They refused worship, yet accepted hospitality. Things excellent on earth are compared with their perfections. Thus the manna of Israel was called "angels' food," or "the bread of the mighty" (Ps. 78:25). Fervid eloquence is likened by Paul to the "tongues of . . . angels" (I Cor. 13:1). The same New Testament word, which designates the resurrection body of the redeemed, describes that habitation which apostate angels lost by sin.

They are also created beings. In Psalm 148 angels are exhorted to "praise the name of the Lord"; because He commanded and they were created, and that by the hand of Jesus Christ. Again do we read:

"Thou, even thou, art Lord alone; thou hast made heaven, the heaven of heavens, with all their host, the earth, and all things that are therein, the seas, and all that is therein, and thou preservest them all; and the host of heaven worshipeth thee" (Neh. 9:6).

"For by him were all things created, that are in heaven, and that are in earth, visible and invisible, whether they be thrones, or dominions, or principalities, or powers; all things were created by him, and for him" (Col. 1:16).

Angels stand in relation to the Lord, as courtiers to a king, and are so mentioned in Job 1:6; and I Kings 22:19.

God's question to Job, "Where wast thou when I laid the foundations of the earth? . . . and all the sons of God shouted for joy" (Job 38:4, 7), lead us to infer that the angels were created sometime before the earth was.

It was a thought with some of the earliest sacred expositors that God took counsel with the angels when He said, "Let us make man in our image." If this were so, then God invited them to participate with Him in man's creation. But for this conclusion we have no authority.

Though called spirits (Ps. 109; Heb. 1:14), this does not prove them to be incorporeal. Man has a spirit (I Thess. 5:23); yet he has a body. That angels have a corporeal nature is rather implied in the words of our Lord, that after the resurrection men shall be like angels (Luke 20:36). It is not more difficult to understand this concerning the angels, than to believe that in their glorified state the redeemed are to exist in "spiritual bodies," as

Paul tells us in his great resurrection argument (I Cor. 15:44). When seen on earth, angels have always appeared youthful and commanding; quite often majestic and awful. Even when so obscured in their personality as to be thought only men, there was a grandeur in their bearing which called forth profound reverence. In their veiled appearances strange overpowering sensations were felt by those who saw them not. This happened to the men with Daniel, and Saul of Tarsus, and the guards about Jesus' tomb (Dan. 10:7; Acts 9:7). Light or splendor usually accompanied them when seen; and the tokens of their presence indicated the power of their personality. Jacob was made a cripple by one touch of an angel's hand. Gideon's offering was consumed by the stroke of an angel's staff. Daniel's men were set quaking at the sound of an angel's voice. Zacharias was struck dumb by the authority of an angel's word. The shepherds were overawed by their glory.

Angels are a company rather than a race. They do not marry, neither do they die. Marriage implies procreation. Procreation meets the necessity of death. The angelic ranks have neither been decreased by death, nor increased by marriage.

It is stated that the redeemed in the resurrection state shall be "equal unto the angels" (Luke 20:36). Therefore, it has been inferred that in their glorified bodies the saints will bear the same nature as angels. But this inference has no other Scripture to sustain it. The term *equal* does not refer to rank or grade, but describes certain deathless conditions which shall then be common to both angels and redeemed. This term, according to classic usage, designated things of proportionate value but different in kind; as, for instance, a wedge of gold from the mine, and a pearl from the ocean.

There is not, then, any authoritative intimation that those who die in the Lord become angels. But there is evidence that such shall finally take precedence above angels by virtue of their union with the Son of God. Of Jesus in the Epistle to the Hebrews it is said:

"Who being the brightness of his glory, and the express image of his person, and upholding all things by the word of his power, when he had by himself purged our sins, sat down on the right hand of the Majesty on high: being made so much better than the angels, as he hath by inheritance obtained a more excellent name than they. For unto which of the angels said he at any time, Thou art my son, this day have I begotten thee? And again, I will be to him a Father, and he shall be to me a Son? And again, when he bringeth in the first begotten into the world, he saith, And let all the angels of God worship him" (Heb. 1:3-6).

And also in our Lord's petition for those who believe on the Son, we have a hint of how exalted their future rank shall be. "Neither pray I for these alone, but for them also which shall believe on me through their word; that they all may be one; as thou, Father, art in me, and I in thee, that they

also may be one in us: that the world may believe
that thou hast sent me. And the glory which thou
gavest me I have given them. . . . Father, I will
that they also, whom thou hast given me, be with
me where I am; that they may behold my glory"
(John 17:20-24).

Scripture divides the present hierarchy of the
heavens into several distinct grades. Mention is made
of seraphim, cherubim, thrones; dominions, mights,
powers; principalities, archangel, angels. What these
governmental terms designate, it is not easy even
to surmise. Great mystery surrounds this administration of the divine Majesty. Eight distinct Greek
words are employed in the New Testament to designate the rank of these heavenly ministers. These
are thus named: *thrones, lordships, principalities,
authorities* (Col. 1:16); *angels, principalities, powers*
(Rom. 8:37); *principalities, authorities, world rul
ers, spiritual powers* (Eph. 6:12). The English reader can easily see when the terms are repeated in
the passages cited. Thrones are greater than lordships; and principalities are apparently higher than
authorities. Eight times the phrase *principalities
and powers* occurs in the English version. And it is
a matter worth careful examination whether in either
instance this refers to holy angelic authority, but
rather to those dominions of demons which are in-
imical to the rule of Jesus Christ, but over which
our Lord holds control.

In Romans 8:37 Paul speaks of some influence
that would separate the redeemed from the love

of God. Surely good angels would never conspire to do this. In Ephesians 6:12 there can be no doubt but the spiritual powers there mentioned are evil, and only evil. And so in Colossians 1:16, it would seem from previous use of the same terms, that *thrones and dominions* (lordships) refer to good angels, while *principalities and powers* (authorities) refer to bad angels. The speculation is interesting, but cannot be made conclusive with the present twilight which surrounds it.

3

CHARACTERISTICS OF ANGELS

THESE INVISIBLE BEINGS are of two orders: the good and the evil. They were not always thus separated. Once all the angels were holy. Being finite and possessing moral liberty, they were tested by temptation. The nature of that test it is impossible to determine as God has not been pleased to divulge the secret. All we know is, that some "sinned," and "kept not their first estate, but left their own habitation," and were "cast down to hell"; "reserved in everlasting chains, under darkness, unto the judgment of the great day" (II Peter 2:4; Jude 6).

Others kept their integrity, and are distinguished in Scripture as "elect angels," "holy ones," "watchers," "ministering spirits" (I Tim. 5:21; Dan. 4:13). Concerning the special sin of the fallen angels, whether it were ambitious pride, as some Scriptures seem to indicate (Isa. 14:13, 14; I Tim. 3:6), or a crime more unnatural and enormous, we shall later consider; but at present we will examine only the characteristics of holy angels.

24

The elect angels are very numerous. It would seem that as far as the heavens transcend the earth in glory and magnitude, by so much do the myriads of angels exceed the multitudes of our globe. And it is a most stupendous and overwhelming thought, that all these are "ministering spirits, sent forth to minister for them who shall be heirs of salvation" (Heb. 1:14).

Two hosts of these met Jacob; hence he called their meeting place Mahanaim. It was a marvelous experience. The man was a coward runaway, carnal and deceitful; yet so precious in the eyes of a patient God that two companies from Heaven's army were sent to defend him. Surely, New Testament followers of the Lamb are not less loved than Jacob (Gen. 32:1, 2).

Moses describes the magnificent attendance on the Lord, when he descended to Sinai, followed by ten thousands of angels (Deut. 33:2). Daniel and John beheld these glorious hosts at home in Heaven, and their number was myriad; a term used in Scripture to designate that which is beyond human computation. And so is the word translated in Hebrews 12:22. "Ye are come . . . to an innumerable company of angels" (Dan. 7:10; Rev. 5:11). Each of the prophets who obtained extensive views of the angels were awed by their vast numbers. David corroborates their testimony. The chariots of God are twenty thousand, even many thousands of angels (Ps. 68: 17). Our Lord in the garden when He said, "Thinkest thou that I cannot beseech my Father, and he shall even now send me more than twelve legions of angels?" (Matt. 26:53), conveys the impression that so numerous were His Father's attendants that to ask a host of seventy-two thousand was only a slight request. As if He said, "For you twelve feeble, unfaithful defenders, my Father can quickly send twelve legions, strong and loyal to Me." One other fact in this connection is more wonderful—love so grand that it constrained Him to forego such succor and meekly submit to the traitor's betrayal that all righteousness might be accomplished!

Wherever mentioned, angels are described as strong, swift, and splendid, subtle as the wind, elastic as the light. To Abraham they came suddenly, without announcement. From Manoah one departed so remarkably that Manoah thereby understood he had seen a vision of God. One walked in the midst of a glowing furnace unharmed. Another condescended to patiently watch in the dark and filthy den of savage beasts. No distance wearies them; and no barriers hinder them. But, though thus above the influences of material circumstances, we nevertheless do read of limitations to their endowments.

1. Their power is limited. When Michael and Satan disputed concerning the body of Moses, the great archangel dared not bring against him an accusation of crime, but referring to authority higher than either, said, "The Lord rebuke thee" (Jude 9).

Again, when in response to Daniel's prayer and fasting on behalf of his nation the angel Gabriel was sent with a message of comfort to him, he encountered an antagonist on the way. And this evil angel of the Persian power withstood Gabriel so stoutly for twenty-one days, that at length it was necessary to dispatch "help" from Heaven. So Michael came to supplement the strength of his fellow angel, and join with him against the persistent foe (Dan. 10:12, 13).

2. Their knowledge is limited. The Lord God has reserved some secrets from His servants. The redemption of fallen man has ever engaged their profoundest curiosity. And though they were employed to announce the Saviour's incarnation, and sang praises at His birth, and defended His feeble infancy, yet they do not appear to have fully comprehended the mystery of it all; and are represented along with human prophets, as anxiously peering down from Heaven with earnest desire to understand the secret of their Lord's humiliation (I Peter 1:10, 11).

The gathering out of an elect Church from both Jews and Gentiles is another wonder to the angels. And very remarkable things are said in reference to this mystery in Ephesians 3:9, 10. There the calling of the Church is represented to be, in the plan of the ages, a school for the angels, that through beholding this congregation of saints on earth, the governments and authorities in Heaven may be educated in the manifold wisdom of God.

For this same reason, because the angels are studying the deportment of the church, Christian women, who may be considered the earthly type of the church of Christ, are exhorted to always display in the assemblies of the saints a token of submission to headship by wearing a covering on the head (I Cor. 11:10).

One other great secret withheld from angels is the time of our Lord's second advent. Though their services on that august occasion shall be more prominent and important than any official work which has been deputed to them in the past, yet the day for that manifestation has not been revealed to them (Matt. 25:31; Luke 9:26; II Thess. 1:7, 10). Said Jesus himself concerning it: "Of that day and hour knoweth no one, not even the angels of heaven" (Matt. 24:36). How conspicuous, then, the folly of those who, making themselves wiser than angels, seek to compute the exact date of Christ's second coming!

3. Scripture gives hints of graded authority among the angels, which each rank maintains with becoming dignity and harmony. Yet only two, Michael and Gabriel, are mentioned by name in the canonical books. And no angel is spoken of by name before the Babylonish captivity. Daniel appears to have been attended by several grades of celestial messengers. The one so terrible, with body like beryl and countenance as the lightning, who stood by the river Hiddekel, was nevertheless secondary to that other designated as the "first chief," who was sent from Heaven to assist the former in his contest with the "prince of . . . Persia" (Dan. 10:13, 14). So much superior was this other angel, in official

dignity if not in strength, that Gabriel says, "I left him there . . . and am come to teach thee."

This same Gabriel, who subsequently announced the birth of the prophet John, spoke of his own peculiar authority, as "that Gabriel who attended in the presence of God" (Luke 1:19). Manifestly some such thought as this was to be impressed on Zacharias: "As you are a priest here in this temple on earth, so am I [Gabriel] likewise a priest in the temple in Heaven. As you, God's oracle, are believed by the people, much more should you believe me, though I declare such extraordinary tidings unto you." Also it appears that some of the angels are connected with warfare, as he who appeared to Gideon (Judges 6:12); some with worship, like him who came to the priest Zacharias (Luke 1:20), and some with punishment, like him whom David saw smiting Jerusalem with pestilence (I Chron. 21:15). There is something peculiarly winsome and familiar in the intercourse which Zechariah the prophet held with angels. There is an entire absence of that consternation, and fear, and splendor which usually accompanied angelic manifestations. Repeatedly does Zechariah say, "I talked with the angel," and "the angel answered me"; till we are led to ask the question, Was that angel a messenger of inferior rank? Or did he designedly adapt himself to the prophet's lowly conditions?

To the Bible student Michael is the most interesting of the angels. Concerning him we have much definite information. Who can read of his "standing," his "contending," his "disputing," his "fighting," his "shouting" on behalf of the people of God, and not realize that he is the champion angel of Israel, sustaining a solitary and unique relationship to that nation, in defiance of all the world powers arrayed against it!

The title *archangel*, applied to Michael, distinguishes him from the Lord Jesus, whom he shall accompany at His second glorious advent. Whether Michael be the only one of his particular rank cannot be certainly determined. The word is never found plural in Scripture. Satan may have been an archangel before he revolted. His name also stands without a fellow in Scripture. There is but one Devil at the head of all demons. And these two mighty beings, seemingly of equal rank, are to meet in command of their respective armies in the great war of Heaven (Rev. 12:7).

To Michael is committed the guardianship of the holy Jewish dead. His name is also connected with the antitypical silver trumpet, which of old summoned detachments from the congregation of Israel, and which at the first resurrection shall call out from the company of the sleepers, all the dead in Christ. So Paul, writing to the Thessalonians, says: "The Lord himself shall descend from heaven with a shout, with the voice of the archangel, and with the trump of God: and the dead in Christ shall rise first" (I Thess. 4:16).

Distinct from Michael is one other of peerless majesty, designated as "the angel of the Lord," "the

messenger of the covenant" (Exod. 3:2; Mal. 3:1).
Contrary to the uniform method of all other angels,
this Angel received intercession from Abraham (Gen.
17:22, 23). Hagar recognized Him as divine (Gen.
16:13; 21:17). In His interview with Moses He appropriated unto Himself that incommunicable title,
"I am that I am." Israel was warned not to provoke
Him, for, said the Lord, "My name is in his inmost";
i. e., "my nature is in his essence" (Exod. 3:14;
23:21). An expression which finds its counterpart in
the confession of the Lord Jesus, "I and my Father
are one"—i. e., one essence (John 10:30). From Joshua He demanded homage (Josh. 5:13-15); unlike the
other angels who always refused it, declaring they
were only "fellow-servants" of the obedient (Rev.
19:10). When Manoah inquired after His name,
this great angel answered, "It is secret," an expression occurring again in Isaiah 9:6, and there unmistakably relating to the incarnate Son—"his name
shall be called Wonderful."

It may be mentioned that Jewish writers quite
uniformly maintain that the phrase, "the angel of the
Lord," relates to the Messiah. But the divine record
is so full on this point that human authorities are
of little necessity. No such meaning, however, can
be attached to the expression, "the angel of the
Lord," in the New Testament. The Authorized Version is misleading here. Let it be noticed that in
every instance where the words occur (nine altogether), the Revisers have changed the reading to

"an angel of the Lord," thus destroying all supposed identity between "the angel" of the Old Testament, and any angel mentioned in the Gospels or Epistles. One exception to this is found in Acts 7:38. There Stephen in his address, referring back to Israel's wilderness history, alludes to that angel, who was, without doubt, Jehovah's messenger of the Presence.

Thus, we gather from the combined testimony of Scripture, that He who visited Israel as the divine Word, in anticipation of the incarnation, ceased to so visit His people after He had become their incarnate Redeemer. We, therefore, read that "God who of old time spoke . . . in divers manners hath at the end of these days spoken unto us in a Son' (Heb. 1:1, 2).

Another distinct order of angels is the cherubim. These number but four. Higher than ordinary angels, their place is nearest the throne; and their service that of ministers extraordinary to the divine Majesty. Their first recorded duty was at Eden, when all the four were deputed to guard the tree of life (Gen. 3:34). Endless theories have been advanced concerning these glorious creatures; but all we know about them is found in Ezekiel 1:4-28; 10:8-22.[1]

---

[1]*Shadow and Substance,* by Geo. C. Needham.

4

THE EMPLOYMENT OF ANGELS

T HIS IS TWOFOLD: heavenly and earthly. In Heaven they minister as priests in the temple of God. Isaiah 6 furnishes a marvelous glimpse of the seraphim, belonging to the higher orders of celestial beings. He saw them ranged in two bands on either side of the throne, singing in responsive chant, one angel sounding across to another, "Holy, holy, holy, is the Lord of hosts!" (Isa. 6:2, 3). The Apocalypse, which abounds in mention of the angels, shows them around the throne, singing, "Worthy is the Lamb"; and before the altar with vials and incense (Rev. 5:11, 12; 8:3, 4). Thus their service in Heaven is connected with worship.

Concerning our earth, from the Creation they have manifested active interest in the affairs of men. The cunning mechanism of this world caused them to shout for joy (Job 38:7). The Sinaitic law, communicated to Moses, was spoken by the mouth of angels (Gal. 3:19). In some wonderful way they

33

operate in nature, having control of nature's laws (Ps. 103:20; 104:4). Their beneficent services are a constant reproach to the demons of Satan, who are ever seeking to destroy the work of God and distort His natural providences.

And it appears from many Scripture intimations that this is a peculiarly important branch of their work. We understand that by means of the good angels the demons are restrained and defeated in their designs to injure the children of God. Were it not so, we do not see how, for one moment, we could be safe from these foul spirits, who are invisible, sly, and overpoweringly numerous. The Christian owes profound and unceasing gratitude to God for this provision of His providence in appointing good angels as our defenders.

Frequently the angels are messengers of punishment. This is not necessarily a degrading office-work. Wind, fire, and pestilence are subservient to them. In their methods they are entirely beyond human inspection or comprehension (I Chron. 21:15, 16, 27). In Psalm 35 they are represented as chasing the wicked with fierce wind, and with darkness causing them to stumble. God said He sent His evil angels into Egypt. It is obvious that they operated through the ten plagues (Ps. 78:49). When Sennacherib defied the armies of the living God, an angel of the Lord, with swift rebuke, descended, and in a single night one hundred and eighty thousand Assyrians became dead men (II Kings 19:35).

The means by which this destruction was accomplished was a simoon, or hot, smothering wind. "Behold, I will send a blast upon him" (II Kings 19:7).

It is quite plain that *the nation and cities of Israel* were, and still are, under angelic guardianship (Dan. 12:1; Ezek. 9:1). Michael is stated to be that great prince set to stand for the Hebrew people. Ezekiel was told to summon those who had charge of Jerusalem. Six of them came, and were sent forth: one to mark and seal all who were faithful in Israel; the others, with their weapons of slaughter to slay every unmarked person in the city.

How far this guardianship now extends to *gentile nations* we do not know. As long as Israel retained a single shred of identity as a government, i. e., till the Shiloh came, angelic interference in their behalf with gentile rulers is clearly to be traced. Nebuchadnezzar's malady and humiliation were certainly directed by an holy one from Heaven. When the great world power passed into the hands of the Medo-Persians, an angel stood to confirm and strengthen Darius in his kingdom (Dan. 11:1). The king of Tyre was called "the anointed cherub who covereth," from which we understand he was a type of that censorship which angels exercise over all human governments. And thus, when the impious Herod, a Roman tool, assumed divine honors, an angel, in vindication of God's glory, immediately smote him a death stroke (Acts 12:22, 23). Cornelius saw an angel interested in his household; and Paul was called to Macedonia by another, who was evidently a guardian angel also (Acts 10:3; 16:9).

But the most certain present fact concerning the angels is their watch-care *of the Church*. It is a marvelous truth, full of sweetness yet full of solemnity, that these innumerable hosts of Heaven are enlisted to serve the saints on earth. The prophetic ladder let down from Heaven, upon which Jacob saw the angels of God ascending and descending, has been appropriated by Jesus unto himself. Communication with Heaven, interrupted by sin, has been restored through Him. For Him who is the Lord of angels, these unseen messengers are ever traveling the shining pathway, bearing gifts and succor from the distant Bridegroom to His bereaved and lonely Bride. As they are His servants, so are they the Church's servants. Though they do not indwell in the saints, like the Holy Spirit, they nevertheless work through external principles, preparing for, confirming and co-operating in the Spirit's ministry. In the vision of the Revelation we behold the four and twenty elders, representing the redeemed, occupying the inner and closest circle around the throne, while the angels stand in the outer and more remote circle (Rev. 5:11).

Their office to the Church is sevenfold:

1. They guide. Philip, the evangelist, was in the midst of a prosperous work in Samaria, when an angel bade him go into the desert. Precisely what for, the angel seems not to have told Philip, but left that for the Spirit of God, as pertaining to His office-work to unfold when the chariot should be reached (Acts 8:26, 29).

When Cornelius was by prayer and fasting seeking after God, the angel appeared and gave him directions how to find the man who should speak words of salvation unto him (Acts 10:2, 3). This was in beautiful accord with the new principle of revelation which the incarnate Son had laid down for His followers, "Ye shall be witnesses unto me" (Acts 1:8). An angel sends the preacher, but refrains testimony himself.

2. They succor. Not only did they feed Israel with manna in the wilderness, and Elijah with bread in the desert (I Kings 19:5, 7), and our Lord after His long fast and sore temptation (Matt. 4:11), but these same thoughtful material offices have been perpetuated this side of the cross as an earnest for our faith. When Paul was shipwrecked, and two hundred and seventy-five souls were in distress with him, we read: "After long abstinence, Paul stood forth in the midst of them, and said, Sirs . . . I exhort you to be of good cheer. . . . For there stood by me this night the angel of God, saying . . . Fear not, Paul . . . Wherefore I pray you to take some meat; for this is for your health; for there shall not a hair fall from the head of any of you" (Acts 27:21-35).

It was an angel of great splendor who strengthened our Lord amid the horrors of Gethsemane. Wrath against sin could not permit of comfort being administered. Hence, mark the words: "There appeared an angel unto him from heaven, strengthening him" (Luke 22:43). And this term is used concerning no other person but the apostle Paul, when his eyesight was restored and he was revived after the prostration attendant upon his extraordinary conversion. One instance of a healing angel is mentioned in John 5:4. How frequently he stirred the Bethesda pool we do not know; but it seemed to have been only at rare intervals since so large a multitude lay waiting so long.

3. They defend. What they did for Jacob in the presence of the estranged and vengeful Esau, and for Daniel in the lions' den, they do for the saints now. Satan spoke truth when he said to Jesus, "He shall give his angels charge concerning thee" (Matt. 4:6). That little children are guarded by angels our Lord has plainly declared. "In heaven their angels do always behold the face of my Father which is in heaven" (Matt. 18:10). Once and again an angel delivered Peter and the other apostles in a most notable manner from prison, "from Herod, and from all the expectations of the Jews" (Acts 5:19; 12:7).

4. They watch the church. This they do in a double sense: for satisfaction; and for protection. It is both a delightful and an appalling thought, that in all the assemblies of believers, there are present angelic onlookers, who are ever curious and sympathetic concerning the matter of our personal salvation. Paul, writing to young Timothy and exhorting him to holy decorum, so charges him, not only for Christ's sake, but because of the elect angels (I Tim. 5:21).

Again, Paul speaking of his own sufferings for Christ, views himself as the "spectacle," or final exhibition of a brutal combat. He invites us to behold him, the center of a vast audience. Men and demons are rejoicing over his agony. But from above he sees the sad, compassionate faces of angels bending down; and that knowledge becomes his motive power to courageous endurance (I Cor. 4:9).

And thus we understand this watchful oversight of angels to be emphasized as the prime reason why Christian women are exhorted to orderly conduct in the church. The angels veil their faces while they worship (I Cor. 11:10). We are told that they greatly fear and reverence as they serve, and hence women, who in the marriage relation are types of that greater union which exists between Christ and the Church, are exhorted to always cover their heads in the public assembly "because of the angels."

5. They have charge of the dead. In the parable of the rich man and Lazarus, and the dying words of Stephen, it is intimated that angels now carry the holy dead to the rest which is part of Paradise. Hebrews 12:22, 23 seems in accord with the same idea. But Scripture quite certainly states that at the resurrection they shall gather all the elect dead for glory and reward (Mark 13:27). As they guarded the tomb and superintended the rising of Jesus, so shall they attend all who are to rise in Him.

6. They shall accompany Christ at His second advent. The future work of the angels shall be vastly more important than their present office of guardian ministry. The combined record of Scripture, apart from the Apocalypse, furnishes us with only a limited

conception of the exaltation of angels. It is not until we behold them in this prophecy, in connection with the revelation of Jesus Christ, that we understand their full grandeur and authority.

Enoch had prophesied, saying, "Behold, the Lord cometh with ten thousand of his saints, to execute judgment upon all" (Jude 14, 15). The passage as found in the Jewish *Book of Enoch*, reads thus: "Behold, he comes with ten thousands of his saints, to execute judgment upon them, and destroy the wicked and reprove all the carnal, for everything which the sinful and ungodly have done and committed against him."

Prophets, evangelists and apostles reiterated the same truth. Each in inspired vision saw Jesus returning, accompanied by innumerable hosts of glorious and mighty angels (Zech. 14:5; Matt. 25:31; Luke 9:26; II Thess. 1:7, 9). The work they shall then perform is tremendous to contemplate. At the awful blast of their trumpets the earth shall disgorge her dead, and the sea cast out her drowned. Before the deafening roar of their voices, the wicked shall shrivel and be scattered as the chaff, while with strong and tender hands they will gather in every distant saint from the four quarters of the world to the shelter and blessedness of the "Father's house." Yet all this is but the beginning of their greatest appointed work.

7. They shall be the executors of judgment. "The Son of man shall send forth his angels, and they shall gather out of his kingdom all things that offend,

and them which do iniquity; and shall cast them into a furnace of fire: there shall be wailing and gnashing of teeth" (Matt. 13:41, 42).

How they are to accomplish this, no human pen dare attempt to delineate. The most fearful imagery of the Bible is to be found in connection with the judgment work of the angels. Among the agents they shall command to execute the wrath of God upon the wicked, we read of fire, hail and blood; the bitterness of wormwood and the darkness of a starless night; plagues of locusts and poisons of scorpions; loathsome ulcers and nauseating brimstone; waters to flood and flames to scorch; impure demons to deceive and unclean beasts to devour; thunders, lightnings and earthquakes; whirlwinds of fury and wine presses of blood. Whether these prophecies be regarded as actuals, or as symbols, either way they teach that the most potent and destructive forces of creation have been delegated to the use of angels, for the punishment of sin at the last day.

RECOGNITION OF ANGELS

O NE CAUTION IS GIVEN US concerning angels. Thrice we are forbidden to pray to them or worship them (Col. 2:18; Rev. 19:10; 22:9). Though so qualified to help, and interested in our salvation, rejoicing when souls are born again and prodigals return, yet intercession is never their office. Only He who was the messenger, Jehovah-Jesus, listened to prayer from the lips of Abraham (Gen. 18:33). In every other case the angels refused homage. To Jesus, in the Father's presence in Heaven, and to the Holy Spirit in the midst of the Church on earth, alone belongs the prerogative of intercession (I John 2: 1, 2; Rom. 8:26).

We have fallen into strangely distorted phases of faith, when the Protestant church practically ignores the ministry of angels, while the Roman Catholic church exalts it into unlawful prominence. This was the fault of Sadducee and Essene. The one sect denied the existence of angels; the other deified their office.

All truth is practical for godliness, though all truth may not be vital to salvation. It is undoubtedly true that Christians lack much of gracious sanctification through indifference to angelic ministry. How comforting to remember that our children, in their daily escapes from the dangers and deaths to which their infantile rashness exposes them, owe their safety to guardian spirits! "That in heaven their angels do always behold the face of my Father" (Matt. 18:10). And surely it is legitimate cause for thanksgiving, when some dread pestilence or tempest sweeps athwart a locality, to recall it was thus aforetime in Egypt, when the destroying angel marked the households of Goshen as God's Passover. So do the angels now tenderly spare those who bear the mark of the atoning blood.

When some otherwise unaccountable barrier checks us in the execution of a rash and possibly wicked purpose, is it not a relief to believe an angel must have done this? Our way was perverse before the Lord like that of Balaam, and God sent His messenger to hinder us (Num. 22:31, 32).

And are we not warranted by Scripture examples of protection, for ascribing our many safe journeys through darkness and through storm, to angelic oversight? Is not Scripture evidence in support of the conclusion that angelic power for locomotion may be swift as harnessed steam or captive electricity? May it not be true that convoys of these strong and splendid beings fly where travel the Lord's own precious and praying ones? Certainly the fact that angels thus protect cannot be set aside, though the method may not be understood.

And if the question were to be raised, Why then do any of the Lord's children suffer peril and calamity? several profitable answers might be advanced. We need be reminded of the continual presence of evil angels, always ready to resist the good angels, and annoy the righteous. We need also to remember our own personal forgetfulness of angelic attention. If we have neither faith nor spiritual interest in angels, can we expect God will find pleasure in sending them to us, undesired? Even the Holy Spirit is limited in power in that heart, or that company of believers where His manifestations are quenched through carnal-mindedness.

But we need also to consider that the Lord has a right to make exceptions to His own laws. He may, for wise purposes of private discipline or public testimony, sometimes decide to withhold His angelic servants from us. Certainly Job was delivered to the cruel handling of demons to teach this same lesson throughout the ages. Peter might have been delivered immediately after the church began praying for him. But God saw fit to hold back His angel for seven days and seven nights till such a volume of agonized and united prayer was provoked that toned up and sanctified the infant church for many a future conflict with the powers of evil.

Surely the cultivation of our souls in fellowship

with angels must lift the aspirations and purify the conduct. The human heart craves some real, though spiritual companionship. This explains the satisfaction found in so-called spiritualism, which is demonology. It is counterfeit angelology. As Christians have been negligent to teach truth concerning angels, the Devil has been active to propagate error concerning departed spirits.

Let us weigh well the benefits to be derived from an unreserved and scriptural faith in the strong and tender offices of these God-appointed messengers of grace. With such companionship and succor at hand, who need fear the loneliness or peril of any earthly circumstance? A Patmos will become a paradise, a prison a palace, and a pillow of stone a pathway of light.

The knowledge, too, of the presence of such watchers and holy ones must produce yet deeper internal results. Solemn fear will grow side by side with calmest peace in the Christian who lives, and acts, and thinks under the conscious restraint of angelic oversight. As they joyfully watch over us to defend, so do they watch over us in grief when we fall into sin. A wholesome shame and loathing of all things unclean and displeasing to them must dwell in the heart which realizes much of their fellowship. And lastly, the dignity of the children of God will be exalted to our apprehension, as it cannot be through any other truth. What are we? What is our destiny? How exceedingly precious unto the Lord every redeemed soul must be, when from His high and holy presence He sends forth these glorious messengers of His majesty to serve and succor us until the day of our manifestation as the Church of the First-born!

THE DEVIL AND HIS DEMONS

THE DISCUSSION under this division must be limited
to the demonology of Scripture. From the earliest
ages of man, the belief has been nearly universal
that mortals could hold converse with beings of or-
ganism and power superior to their own. Men, under
all conditions, have manifested a desire to break
through the mysterious bound which the Creator
has established between the material and spiritual
worlds. The fallen sons of Adam have blindly confessed their need of a helper and guide wiser than
themselves; yet, with the perverse instincts of a sinful nature, they have invariably turned away from
God's own authorized revelation and sought counsel
through forbidden channels.

Hundreds of volumes have been written recording
cases of demonology, witchcraft, spiritual ecstasy,
and modernized spiritualism. These histories are foul,
startling, and absurd. Nor would they be worthy of
attention here, only that so many of the incidents

seem fully authenticated. Yet it is difficult to comprehend how men and women of average common sense could have been deceived by such silly and fictitious pretensions to supernatural communication.

On the other hand, many books have been written in the interest of science to prove that all such cases of the apparently supernatural were attributable to one of four primary causes: sleight of hand, sensorial deception, mental disease, or hypnotism. And while such scientific and psychical efforts have accomplished immense and wholesome results in tearing to tatters the veil of superstition, which, alas! enwraps not a few of us all, yet many of these writings have wrought incalculable mischief in that they have flung to the winds of contempt with godless hand those actual divine mysteries which though ridiculed are not explained to the satisfaction of the thoughtful and honest mind.

With weariness and disgust the intelligent Christian, enlightened by the Spirit of God, turns from the distorted testimony of men to that one Book which alone casts reasonable light upon this most fascinating, dangerous, and awful truth: *the presence and power of Satan in the earth.*

The doctrine of demons, though abundantly and decisively taught in Scripture, is yet in all instances attended with obscurity. If we attempt to trace a connected history of the fallen angels, from their first apostasy to their final doom, we find ourselves constantly bewildered by the abrupt and fragmentary character of the testimony concerning them.

In the opening pages of the Bible we are permitted to look upon the picture of an innocent and happy pair in the Garden of Eden. Peace, purity, and perfection everywhere prevail. Suddenly an adversary appears upon the scene, and directly there is a resultant transformation of all this loveliness into sin, curse, and chaos. We are stirred to ask the question, "Whence comest thou, Satan?" Promptly he replies, "From walking up and down in the earth as a spy." But as this answer supplies no tangible information, we perceive that we are dealing with one of the profoundest mysteries of the universe.

We turn onward the leaves of holy Scripture, and are permitted to behold another scene: the vision is Heaven, with the Lord of glory seated upon His throne of majesty, surrounded by dreadful living creatures, and hosts of holy angels standing on His right hand and on His left, to do His bidding. A question of momentous interest concerning the Israel on earth comes up in that august council: "Who shall persuade [deceive] Ahab, that he may go up and fall at Ramoth-gilead? And there came forth a spirit and stood before the Lord and said, I will persuade him. And the Lord said unto him, Wherewith? And he said, I will go forth and be a lying spirit in the mouth of all his prophets" (I Kings 22:19-22).

Now, we are perfectly certain that no unfallen angel could have volunteered his services in so foul a manner. None but a demon would have offered to become a lying spirit. He evidently belonged to the ranks of him who is the "father of lies," and "abode not in the truth." In amazement we then ask another question: "What means this strange access into the court of Heaven? How can the purity of God tolerate the proximity and suggestions of these evil ones?" But Scripture gives us no answer. The Holy Spirit suddenly closes the rift in the clouds of heavenly mystery which he had so briefly drawn asunder, and we are reminded we are bound to believe, and wait while we believe, until it shall be granted us to "know even as we are known."

There is yet another reason why the doctrine of demons is so difficult to apprehend. Satan's master stroke of policy is to divert our minds from inquiry concerning his true character and the methods by which he governs his kingdom. His resources are so varied and his modes of operation so elastic that it is extremely difficult to determine the bounds of his authority. Sometimes he employs the vehicle of darkness to blind the minds of those who do not believe, lest the light of the Gospel of the glory of Christ should dawn upon them (II Cor. 4:4). And sometimes, unto those who do believe the Gospel, he transforms himself into an angel of light, that thus, by bewildering, he may delude them into his snares (II Cor. 11:14).

7

THE DIGNITY OF SATAN

SATAN PERSONALLY, rather than demons, is dealt with in Scripture.

This is a leading fact to be carefully noted. Very little can be learned of demons apart from the prince of demons. Sometimes the name Satan stands generic for all fallen angels. As for instance, "If Satan cast out Satan, he is divided against himself" (Matt. 12:26). This clearly refers to demons (*damonia*), who are the agents employed, rather than to *ho Diabolos*, the personal Devil. Thus in studying the subject we must always bear in mind that we are confronting a compacted unity. Our Lord, addressing the unclean spirit who tormented the man in the tombs, asked him, "What is thy name? And he answered, saying, My name is Legion, for we are many" (Mark 5:9).

Satan rules a rebel kingdom.

This is a second important fact to note. And this fact puts the whole host of demons in unique posi-

tion in the universe of God, and distinguishes them
from all other created spiritual intelligences. The
holy angels have no kingdom. They are spoken of as
"princes, ministers, messengers, servants," but always
in relation to God, their King and head, to whom
they are loyal. Never do we read of the good angels
acting independently of God's will. Our Lord taught
us to pray, "Thy will be done in earth, as in heaven."
Repeatedly does the following form of expression
occur in Scripture: "My God hath sent his angel"
(Dan. 6:22; Rev. 22:16). Thus incidentally the
obedience of the righteous angels is emphasized and
contrasted with the disobedience of the evil angels.

In distinction, then, to the good angels, who de-
light in subjection to divine rule, the demons are
revolters. The manifestation of this rebellion is a
mimic kingdom, wherein Satan, as head of an organ-
ized administration for promoting spiritual wickedness, reigns as prince of darkness (Matt. 12:24-26).
All Scriptures bearing on the subject show that the
evil spirits are very numerous. The expression, "The
angels which kept not their first estate" denotes this;
while the term *principalities*, found in Ephesians
6:12, and several other places, designates their great
power. Their first estate, like that of every other
creature made, was holiness and happiness. The
Bible is reserved as to the time or circumstance of
their apostasy. It is hard to determine what sinful
lapse had occurred previous to that manifestation of
transgression which culminated in the Deluge, for
plainly the apostate angels were involved in the

judgment of the Flood (II Peter 2:4, 5). Job and his friend Eliphaz surely spake with deeper intention than merely to point their arguments with strong oriental comparison when they declared: "He put no trust in his servants; and his angels he charged with folly. . . . Yea, the heavens are not clean in his sight" (Job 4:18; 15:15). The writer of the Hebrews may also have had in view the same fact of angelic transgression, when he by inspiration wrote, "It was therefore necessary that the patterns of things in the heavens, should be purified with these [the blood of bulls and goats]; but the heavenly things themselves, with better sacrifices than these" (Heb. 9:23). Not that we are to understand for one moment that any provision has been made for the atonement of fallen angels, but that, as under the symbolic Mosaic ritual, the holy tabernacle itself and all its furniture was purged with blood; so, perhaps, this profound passage teaches that there must be also some purging of the things of Heaven from the defilement of wicked spirits.

It seems plain that Satan had some connection with the earth and its occupants before man appeared. And also that Satan had already fallen. If, as appears to be hinted in the Epistles (I Tim. 3:6; James 3:15), pride, or jealousy, was the cause of the "condemnation of the devil," and if Satan were once God's vice-regent over the earth, we are able to trace a fairly well connected chain of evidence as to the reasons which led him to tempt our first parents in Eden.

Satan was envious of man as his successor. For God had said, "Let man have dominion over all the earth, and over every living thing that moveth upon the earth" (Gen. 1:26-28). We are strengthened in these conclusions when we turn to the Gospels and read His proposals to the second Adam, who came to undo the mistake of the first Adam: "The devil taketh him up unto an exceeding high mountain, and showeth him all the kingdoms of the world, and the glory of them; and he saith unto him, All these things will I give thee, if thou wilt fall down and worship me" (Matt. 4:8, 9). The bitter disappointment which Satan had cherished for prolonged ages culminated in utter desperation as he beheld the priceless honor of earth's dominion about to slip from his grasp forever. He knew he was finally doomed. He seemed not to care for that, could he just for one moment taste the unfathomable satisfaction in the homage he once knew as Lucifer, son of the morning, and have the Son of God, the incarnate Man, the Lord of angels, bow the knee and say, "I worship thee."

The expression, *ho Diabolos*—the Devil—stands alone among *damonia*, for there is but one Devil, though there are legions of demons. How great he was, and how great he still is in his wretched apostasy, we learn from one circumstance. When Michael the archangel disputed with him about the body of Moses, we are told he dare not bring against him a charge of crime. Not simply that angelic grace caused Michael to refrain from a railing judgment, but, recognizing Satan's still permitted dignity, he dared not insult him (Jude 6). Among the very few things which God names as great in Scripture is designated "the great dragon . . . called the Devil, and Satan" (Rev. 12:9). Peter also refers to the reverence paid to the fallen angels. Self-willed, daring men, he says, speak evil of dignitaries (apostate glories); but powerful and holy angels "bring not railing accusation against them before the Lord" (II Peter 2:11). *INTERESTING*

There are two interesting passages in the prophecies, severally applied to the king of Babylon and the king of Tyre: "How art thou fallen from heaven, O Lucifer [Daystar], son of the morning! how art thou cut down to the ground, which didst weaken the nations! For thou hast said in thine heart, I will ascend into heaven, I will exalt my throne above the stars of God: I . . . will ascend above the heights of the clouds; I will be like the most High" (Isa. 14:12-14).

"Thus saith the Lord God; Thou sealest up the sum [or pattern], full of wisdom, and perfect in beauty. Thou hast been in Eden the garden of God. . . . Thou art the anointed cherub that covereth; and I have set thee so. . . . Thou wast perfect in thy ways from the day that thou wast created, till iniquity was found in thee" (Ezek. 28:12-15).

These Scriptures, though strongly colored with Jewish imagery, and doubtless earthly and national in their first application, must nevertheless have ulterior reference to the former glory of Satan. Of

FORMER GLORY

no earthly king of Tyre, or any other monarchy, of
no precursor of the Antichrist, or final man of sin,
could it be truly said, "Thou sealest up the sum
[pattern], full of wisdom, and perfect in beauty. . . .
Thou wast perfect in thy ways from the day that
thou wast created till iniquity [unrighteousness]
was found in thee."

The words of our Lord are in confirmation of this:
"He said unto them, I beheld Satan as lightning fall
from heaven" (Luke 10:18). Alford, called the
"prince of critics," says the figure, lightning falling,
refers not to the suddenness, but to the glorious
brightness of him who fell.

8

THE SPHERE OF DEMONS

WE ARE LED TO INFER from our Lord's statement (John 8:44), reiterated by His apostle (I John 3:8), that the demons fell from holiness very soon after they were created. "Ye are of your father the devil. . . . He was a murderer from the beginning, and abode not in the truth." "He that committeth sin is of the devil; for the devil sinneth from the beginning." Whatever ages of the past may be condensed into the phrase, "the beginning," it is certain that it always designates a period of unfathomable antiquity (John 1:1-3).

Promptness of action seems to stamp his infernal methods. Perhaps Adam had only been created three days, and Eve a shorter time, when the temptations of the serpent were applied to them. On the sixth day man was created; on the seventh, God rested from all His works which He had made. At the beginning of the new week Adam gave names to all the living creatures; but for Adam, among them all,

57

"there was not found an helpmeet for him." Then, probably that same night following the man's first working day, the Lord God caused a deep sleep to fall upon Adam; and during his sleep took from his side one of his ribs, of which the Lord builded a woman for the man. Very speedily, it would seem, came the solicitation of the tempter and the quick overthrow. A passage in the Psalms seems to have reference to Adam's sudden fall. "Nevertheless man being in honor abideth not" (Ps. 49:12). That is, as Alexander paraphrases it, "He lodges not for a single night in this condition of uprightness."

Whenever and however the first departure from allegiance to their Creator occurred, we do know that now the apostate angels are vagabonds, free, yet bound. According to old English statutes a vagabond is defined as "one without a home; they wake on the night and sleep on the day; they haunt detestable places; and no man knows from whence they came, nor whither they go." Sometimes we read of demons in the "heavenly places" (Eph. 6:12); sometimes "in the air" (Eph. 2:2); sometimes "in the earth" (Job 1:7); sometimes "in the sea" (Matt. 8:32); sometimes "in the bodies of men" (Matt. 12:43); sometimes in "waterless places" (Luke 11:24); sometimes "in swine" (Mark 5:13); sometimes "in the kings of the earth" (Rev. 16:14). Having left their own habitation, they are "reserved in chains under darkness unto the judgment" (Jude 6).

What relation the darkness of this world sustains to their chain of bondage, it may be difficult to fully grasp. Compared with the glory and brightness of the abode which they left, the atmosphere of this globe, one-half of which is always shrouded in literal night, is certainly darkness to demons. But there seems to be a moral sense in which Scripture employs the term *darkness* to express seven distinct ideas.

1. A secret place. "What I tell you in darkness, that speak ye in light; and what ye hear in the ear, that preach ye upon the housetops" (Matt. 10:27).

2. For error or ignorance. "The Gentiles, unto whom now I send thee [Paul], to open their eyes, and to turn them from darkness to light, and from the power of Satan unto God" (Acts 26:17, 18).

3. For punishment. "When I looked for good, then evil came unto me: and when I waited for light, there came darkness" (Job 30:26).

4. For calamity. "And they shall look unto the earth; and behold trouble and darkness, dimness of anguish; and they shall be driven to darkness" (Isa. 8:22).

5. For Hell, the place of misery. "He will keep the feet of his saints, but the wicked shall be silent in darkness" (I Sam. 2:9).

6. For the veil of God's glory. "And it came to pass, when ye heard the voice out of the midst of the darkness, (for the mountain did burn with fire,) that ye came near unto me" (Deut. 5:23).

7. For extreme remoteness from the presence and favor of the Lord. "Cast ye the unprofitable servant

into outer darkness: there shall be weeping and gnashing of teeth" (Matt. 25:30).

Each of these seven distinct ideas of the term *darkness* may contribute one link to the perfect chain of that bondage in which pending justice now detains the fallen spirits. For we do know that they are held under a sevenfold condition: in retreat, in disgrace, in error, in misery, in rebellion, remote from divine favor, yet reserved unto final doom. We are inclined to decide, however, that we are not, in either of the two instances where the word *chain* occurs, to understand it according to its modern significance. Two Greek words are employed. The first means a pit or cavern, and is so rendered by some oldest Manuscripts (II Peter 2:4). The second is a word of considerable latitude, and not only designates the fetter by which anything is bound, but any impediment to liberty (Jude 6). Some of the apostate angels may yet be free to haunt the air and earth; while others, guilty of higher crimes, may now be shut up in dark caverns of detention till the final judgment.

A passage from the Apocryphal *Book of Enoch* has much interest in this connection: "Therefore was he offended with them [angels] and bound them until the period of the consummation of their crimes, in the secret year. I beheld . . . a desolate spot prepared and terrific. There, too, I beheld seven stars of heaven bound in it together. . . . These are those of the stars which have transgressed the commandment of the most high God; and are here bound, until the infinite number of the days of their crimes be completed" (18:16; 87:2, 3).

In its simplest sense, the word *Satan* means an adversary. Conformed to this idea, apart from personal reference to the arch demon, we find the term so used repeatedly in Scripture. David said of Joab and Abishai, his sister's children, "What have I to do with you, ye sons of Zeruiah, that ye should this day be adversaries [satans] unto me?" (II Sam. 19:22). In the same secondary sense, Paul three times uses the word *Devil;* in such language exhorting Christian women "that they be not false accusers" (*diaboloi*) (I Tim. 3:11; II Tim. 3:3; Titus 2:3).

The distinguishing personal titles of Satan, the Devil, are these: tempter, dragon, wicked one, Beelzebub, prince of this world, god of this world, Apollyon. In addition, as descriptive of his craft and boldness, he is called that old serpent the Devil, and that roaring lion the Devil.

It is quite plain from Scripture that Satan has assumed royal divine honors toward the heathen world. Whole nations paid him homage. This is the explanation of Jehovah's stern repression of idolatry. He was "provoked to jealousy with strange gods, with abominations provoked they him to anger. They sacrificed unto devils, not to God" (Deut. 32: 16, 17).

Paul corroborates this statement of Moses, and affirms "that the things which the Gentiles sacrifice, they sacrifice to devils, and not to God" (I Cor. 10:20).

FALSE GODS
IDOLATRY

Thus the root offense of idolatry was demonology. All its stupidity and senseless ceremony were but addenda to the main fact. The senses were gratified, the passions unloosed, the conscience deluded—but chief over all, Satan was worshiped.

While thus Satan has ever assumed the attitude of lordship toward the heathen world, to the children of God his most frequent and favorite relationship is that of accuser. According to ancient oriental usage, an accuser was a judicial adversary in constant attendance upon the court of a monarch as the appointed agent of punishment. This accuser received his emoluments from the spoils of criminals; hence, he rejoiced in their condemnation. He was also an official spy. His prerogative allowed him to lay temptations and snares in the way of those culprits whom he hoped afterward to see punished for his own aggrandizement.

With this historical meaning of the word *accuser* in mind, we perceive the marvelous suitableness of some of Paul's sayings. As for instance: "To whom ye forgive anything . . . forgave I it in the person of Christ, lest Satan should get an advantage of us: for we are not ignorant of his devices" (II Cor. 2:11).

In this same connection it is a noteworthy coincidence that among the numerous records of witchcraft preserved we find no other technical term so often recurring as the epithet *accused*, which was invariably applied to those supposed to be under satanic influences.

In Job's time Satan boldly presented himself in

the presence of God as man's accuser. Just how much
of that former liberty is at present allowed him we
do not know. The ascension of our Lord, as the
Advocate of His saints, has certainly taken away
Satan's former official standing in Heaven's judicial
court. That he still accuses and slanders the saved
we cannot doubt, though in some restricted manner
as compared with his former freedom. A very remarkable word is used in Hebrews 9:24 in connection
with the priesthood of Jesus. "Christ . . . is entered
into heaven, now to appear in the presence of God
for us." This word *appear (emphanizo)* is not the
same as the two other words translated "appear" in
verses 26 and 28. Here it is a legal and official term.
In every instance where it is found in the New
Testament, it is associated with personal authority.
It dignifies the whole passage, and makes it teach
this: Jesus Christ has gone into Heaven on official
business on behalf of His people. What that official
business is we will let the apostle John explain: "If
any man sin, we have an advocate with the Father,
Jesus Christ the righteous." "For this purpose the Son
of God was manifested, that he might destroy the
works of the devil. . . . He that is begotten of God
keepeth [preserveth] himself, and that wicked one
toucheth him not" (I John 2:1; 3:8; 5:18).

The complete casting out of Satan and his hosts
from some place of heavenly access had not certainly
been accomplished in Paul's day, for he by the Spirit
of inspiration asserted: "We wrestle not against flesh
and blood, but against principalities, against powers,

against the rulers of the darkness of this world, against spiritual wickedness in high [heavenly, celestial] places" (I Cor. 15:40; Eph. 6:12).

The Apocalypse looks onward to a time when this casting down will be done, and the holy residents in Heaven shall shout: "Now is come salvation, and strength, and the kingdom of our God, and the power of his Christ: for the accuser of our brethren is cast down, which accused them before our God day and night" (Rev. 12:10).

It seems further plain that this complete casting out of Satan from opportunity for accusation in the heavenlies lies at least as far onward as the end of this Gospel age: for we read that those who overcame his slanders did so "by the blood of the Lamb," an expression which unmistakably links the accusations of Satan to this present age.

With great comfort for the believer, the closing of the eighth chapter of Romans combines the double fact of a present accuser and a powerful advocate. In a freer translation: "Who shall lodge an accusation against them whom God hath chosen? God who acquitteth? Who is he who shall condemn? Christ who died? Rather indeed who is raised up, who is actually at the right hand of God, and who maketh intercession for us. Who shall separate us from the love of Christ? . . . I am persuaded that neither death, nor life, nor angels, nor principalities, nor powers, nor things present, nor things to come, nor height, nor depth, nor any other created being shall be able to separate us from the love of God which is in Christ Jesus our Lord" (Rom. 8:33-38).

The whole point here of Paul's satirical questionings is to the intent that he may emphasize the fact that while there does exist an adversary, malicious and ever-anxious to "lodge accusations" against the children of God, yet he is a defeated and restrained foe; since One stronger than he has entered into the court and presence of God, where now He continually abides to make intercession for the saints, and confront Satan with the great acquittal which His atoning death has accomplished.

9

GENERAL METHODS OF DEMONS

V ERY EARLY in the Biblical history it is implied
that fallen man held communication with the evil
spirits, and that such intercourse was sinful for both
parties and exceedingly displeasing to God. The
facts are darkly stated in briefest language, and
we must examine them with cautious reverence, lest
our imaginations be tempted to supply what is lack-
ing in the narrative.

Thus we read, "And it came to pass, when men
began to multiply on the face of the earth, and
daughters were born unto them, that the sons of
God saw the daughters of men that they were fair;
and they took them wives of all which they chose. . . .
There were giants in the earth in those days; and
also after that, when the sons of God came in unto
the daughters of men, and they bare children to
them, the same became mighty men which were of
old, men of renown. And God saw that the wickedness of man was great in the earth, and that every

imagination of the thoughts of his heart was only evil continually. And it repented the Lord that he had made man on the earth, and it grieved him at his heart" (Gen. 6:1-6).

The question of paramount interest in this connection is, Who are meant by the "sons of God"? If, as many Bible students have supposed, the expression relates only to the seed of Seth, who were in the line of God's chosen purposes and as such called sons of God, in distinction to men who are claimed to be the seed of Cain, then this whole paragraph of Scripture has nothing whatever to do with demonology, and we may immediately dismiss it as irrelevant evidence.

But there are some difficulties involved in this theory, and it is necessary to confront them. The revelations of God lose nothing of their power by being submitted to severe scrutiny. The women, be it observed, are all classed as "daughters of men," in whichever line their pedigree may have run; yet the men are supposed to represent two Adamic branches. It is not fair thus to degrade the whole of womankind, since she is elsewhere stated in Scripture to be man's fellow-heir of the grace of life (I Peter 3:7). The contrast is plainly between the sons of God and daughters of Adam as the generic head of all, without specific reference to either Cain or Seth. There can be no doubt who the women were. They were earthly creatures, descendants of Adam and Eve. Squarely then arises the question, Who are meant by "sons of God"? No opinion must be ventured. We will let the light of God's Word guide us as far as it will. This expression, "sons of Elohim," is found but seven times in the Old Testament; five times it is translated "sons of God," and twice so given in the marginal readings of the Revised Version. In Job 1:6 we find the third occurrence of this phrase, "Now there was a day when the sons of God came to present themselves before the Lord"; so also in Job 2:1, where the words are the same.

There cannot be any reasonable doubt as to the meaning of these passages. The scene is Heaven; the place the court of the Lord's royal majesty. The "sons of God," with Satan among them, are angelic beings, creatures who are admitted near enough to the presence of God for Him to be represented as conversing with them. They could not have been righteous men from the earth, for while we are told in Scripture that the Lord sometimes came down and talked with men (Num. 11:17; Deut. 5:24), we are never told that men went up to Heaven to talk with God. John informs us: "No man hath seen God at any time" (John 1:18; 3:13). This alone should be conclusive evidence that these "sons of God" could not have been any of the seed of Adam.

Again the Book of Job furnishes the fifth occurrence of the phrase: "Gird up now thy loins like a man; for I will demand of thee, and answer thou me. Where wast thou when I laid the foundations of the earth? . . . When the morning stars sang together, and all the sons of God shouted for joy?" (38:3-7). There cannot be less certainty regarding the mean ing of this passage. Critics may quibble if they wish over the imagery of the words; one fact they cannot neutralize—these sons of God could not have been men, since they were some order of beings existing previous to men. The point and the taunt of God's logic lies in the question, "Where wast thou?" since neither Job nor one of Adam's race was born when the Creator, taking counsel of Himself, planned the world and then spread out its completed glories for the admiration of His angels.

No more does the phrase occur in the Authorized Version of the Old Testament; but it is found again twice in the original. "Give to Jehovah, ye sons of the mighty, give to Jehovah honor and strength" (Ps. 29:1). The word translated "mighty" is the plural form of one of the names which designate the omnipotence of God. We must not degrade it from its loftiness by using it for an attribute of men.

The seventh and last place is also in the Psalms. "For who, in the sky, can compare to Jehovah? Who is like to Jehovah among the sons of the mighty?" (Ps. 89:6, "sons of God," R. V. marg.). The scene of this magnificent challenge is in the sky. The whole of the context asserts a strong declaration that there is no one to be compared with the Lord, even among those orders of creation which are superior to man. It is a question addressed to the exalted inhabitants of Heaven, and thus identifies the "sons of the mighty" as none other than those creatures whose rank is intermediate between Jehovah and men.

Since then, as is clearly obvious, in five out of seven occurrences the phrase "sons of God" designates angelic intelligences, what would rationally be the conclusion regarding these terms in Genesis 6: 2, 4? Must not the reference there be to angels also, though certainly to apostate ones, as their conduct indicates?

The gravest of difficulties now appears. How could these apostate angels (*Nephilim*), being spiritual, have union with the daughters of men? We do not know. Neither do we understand how good angels who are spiritual, materialized or etherealized at will, and partook of material forms of food with Abraham and others; nor how they pulled Lot by the hand; nor how seven impure spirits could inhabit one human body. Being greater than mankind, they are superior to those barriers by which matter hampers men. It is affirmed of the elect angels who have passed their probation and seem no longer under the liability of sinning, that "they neither marry nor are given in marriage." But such exalted conditions are not declared of the apostate angels. One fact is manifest; throughout their fragmentary history, all their doings, after some fashion, connect them with the bodies of human beings, to dishonor, abuse, or destroy them.

The offspring of these mysterious unions between Nephilim and "daughters of men" were a race of giants, Gibborim and Rephaim. The Gibborim were noted for their impiety (Num. 13:33; Deut. 25:18, 19). The Rephaim are associated with the dead or the ghosts of the dead. "Hell [the grave] from beneath is moved for thee to meet thee at thy coming: it stirreth up the dead [Rephaim] for thee, even all the chief ones of the earth. . . . They shall speak and say unto thee, Art thou also become weak as we? art thou become like unto us?" (Isa. 14:9, 10).

It seems pertinent to here insert another quotation from the Apocryphal *Book of Enoch*. It is at least valuable as giving us a tradition of great antiquity regarding the sin of the apostate angels. Without doubt the author of this book was a sober, God-fearing man. The coincidences between the *Book of Enoch* and the inspired Epistles of James, II Peter, and Jude are so marked as to lead to the conclusion that these men knew and respected the reputed prophecy of Enoch in their day. And while the words of Enoch supply fuller detail than the inspired writings, there is no clash of statement between them. In this book we read: "It happened after the sons of men had multiplied in those days, that daughters were born to them elegant, beautiful. And when the angels, the sons of heaven beheld them, they became enamored of them, saying to each other: Come, let us select for ourselves wives from the progeny of men, and let us beget children" (7:1, 2).

"Therefore I made not wives for you [angels], because being spiritual, your dwelling is in heaven" (15:7).

"The valley of the angels who had been guilty of seduction, burned underneath its soil. . . . The waters will be changed, and become a fire which shall blaze forever" (66:6, 15).

"Those who seduced them shall be bound with chains forever" (68:39; see II Peter 2:4, 5).

"Behold they committed crimes, laid aside their class, and intermingled with women. With them also they transgressed; married with them, and begot children. A great destruction therefore shall come upon the earth; a deluge, a great destruction shall take place in one year" (comp. 21:2, 3; 87:2, 3).

There is a marvelous analogy which is patent, though not explainable, between our Lord's incarnation and the development of the final Antichrist. Jesus, though born of a virgin, was begotten of the Holy Ghost, a God-man. The Antichrist, who is in all respects to be His infamous counterpart, shall be a demon-man, the son of perdition (II Thess. 2:3). The incarnation, which was the foundation and joy of Christian faith, was at the same time the target for the ridicule and blasphemy of the unbelieving world. The claims of Jesus of Nazareth to a divine-human origin were distorted and scandalized. Yet to so foul a spirit as Satan this was a fortunate circumstance, and thus Scripture intimates that he will not overlook it in establishing his chain of assumptions to the false messiahship of the last Antichrist. This man of sin, energized by the Devil, must have a mimic incarnation, as he is also to have a mimic resurrection (Rev. 13:3), "that all who dwell upon the earth shall worship him, whose names are not written in the book of life" (Rev. 13:8).

Shall we then cry, Impossible! to the demoniacal

atrocities recorded in Genesis when more remarkable satanic wonders are prophesied in the Apocalypse? As earth's agonized dispensation of sin was inaugurated with acts of supernal wickedness, so shall its approaching close be characterized by miraculous lying wonders. The marvels of modern spiritualism need not surprise us. They are to constitute a leading feature of latter-day demonism.

10

PARTICULAR METHODS WITH
THE WORLD

It will be proper, in tracing out the methods of satanic working, to keep distinct what the Bible clearly separates: namely, his double attitude toward the saint and sinner, the Church and the world. He wears a twofold aspect, and tempts in a twofold manner each of these two great moral classes. This thought will be developed in order as we proceed.

Satanic methods with the world. The cult of Satan is manifold and intricate. With the intellectual and cultured he operates through mysteries. With the coarse and ignorant he appeals to the senses through wonders and superstitions. Yet one word characterizes all demonology: Foul! Foul! Every history of devil-traffic shows the rites of demonology to be not only profligate, but disgustingly loathsome. It was common among witches and wizards, as late as the seventeenth century, to rob the graves of little infants and use their bones in making magic salves. They mimicked the ordinances of the Christian church; kept a Sabbath of devilish revelry; required their patrons "to be baptized in their own blood, in Satan's great name"; and made toads, serpents, and the most revolting of reptiles the channels of their augury.

It has always been the primary object of demons to annoy and injure the bodies of men. Having no bodies of their own since their apostasy, they have special liking for the bodies of men. Hence, the unclean spirit mentioned in Matthew's Gospel who went out of a man, and, walking through dry places seeking rest and finding none, took unto himself seven other wicked spirits worse than he, and they, entering in, dwelt again in the man, and his last state was worse than his former (Matt. 12:43-45). To them a swine's body is preferable to no habitation; thus the legion besought Jesus not to send them to the abyss (not simply the deep, or ocean) before their time, but into the swine (Mark 5:12).

With this passion for hurting men always influencing the deeds of impure spirits, we find them impelling those in league with them to use poisons, charms, evil eyes, incantations, and various mystical rites to harm the life, limb, or goods of those who were supposed to be under their control. Hence, the man out of the tombs whom Jesus met was always day and night cutting himself with stones (Mark 5:5).

Those who read the statutes and enactments of civil law for the suppression of witchcraft during the Middle Ages will be horrified at the atrocities perpetrated in the name of judgment. But, whatever of justice or injustice these court records reveal, one mighty feature towers above all others. Satan in every instance accomplished his main object, that of harming men's bodies. Whoever in any degree countenanced or patronized the insinuations of his satanic majesty paid the price in most fearful and ingeniously devised sufferings. The atrocities of demonology exceed the horrors of the papal inquisition. Innocent men and women were tortured by hundreds till they at last fraudulently confessed league with the imps.

Whole communities of little children in Germany, Switzerland, and Scotland were goaded on to false confession. They were buried to the neck in pits, they were anchored in winter-cold waters, they were thrust into torturing machines, they were stuck with pins, they were dragged after horses, they were made to swallow quantities of pins and vomit them up, their finger nails were drawn out with pincers and pins inserted in their places, they were stripped naked and dishonored to make them reveal the "witch mark" upon their bodies. After such tortures, if they did not die under them, they were hanged or burned.

No inquisitor of Rome ever assumed more infernal authority than did the notorious Matthew Hopkins, the Witchfinder General, who resided in Essex,

England, about the year 1644. His practices reduced judicial cruelty to a loathsome fine art. And here should be noted one very remarkable fact. The martyrs of Jesus Christ most rarely recanted. Their dying testimony was a triumph of sweetness, loyalty, and rapture. But the martyrs of Satan almost invariably witnessed a double confession of truth and falsehood. One moment they protested their innocence; the next, as if impelled by a power foreign to themselves, they acknowledged their complicity with demons. And this was repeated again and again in hundreds of cases, till no reliance whatever could be placed upon the dying words of those supposed to be under the spell of the Evil One.

There are medical men living today, of admirable good sense and extensive research, whose one fault seems to be their disbelief in Scripture record, who are asserting that cases of so-called "possession" were nothing more than insanity or epilepsy. We are thankful to have no controversy with such. Betwixt us there is a great gulf fixed. In company with evangelists and apostles, we stand upon the mountaintop of God's inspired revelation, from which we look down with profoundest sadness upon that pitiable "wisdom of men" which has left God and the supernatural out of its reasonings.

Our Lord Jesus clearly made a distinction between demoniacal possession and forms of disease. The very formula He used in His great commission to the twelve and seventy decides this: "Heal the sick, cleanse the lepers, raise the dead, cast out devils"

(Matt. 10:8). Let us observe the rise in the gradation of responsibility. "The sick" were those not hopelessly so. "The lepers" were incurables. "The dead" were certainly beyond human skill. The case "with devils" was put as paramount in difficulty to the others. Take another statement of the commission made by Luke, who was himself an accredited physician, and would hardly have needed to make a pathological blunder, even if prejudiced in favor of Jesus. "He gave them power and authority over all devils, and to cure diseases" (Luke 9:1).

It is this same physician Luke who particularized in the case of the father's only child: "Jesus rebuked the unclean spirit, and healed the child, and delivered him again to his father" (Luke 9:42).

This record, compared with the account in Mark 9:27, develops a fact of additional interest. The indwelling of demons was accompanied in frequent cases with a simulation of disease, such as blindness, deafness, and extreme hysteria. So all the accounts in the Gospels describe a double action performed. First, the demons were spoken to with authority and commanded to vacate. Then the wounded, exhausted, half-dead creature, so lately possessed, was lifted, vitalized, soothed and restored healed to his relatives.

It is in this connection we are to notice that four prime sins are charged against Satan and his hosts in the Word of God: *lying, murder, malice, pride*.

With these four propensities impelling them, their highest joy seems to be in leading unwary souls

into those circumstances where they shall be in-
duced to commit crime. Thus we read of them under
God's providential permission as trying the integrity
of men's souls. Holy angels are also, without doubt,
employed by God as His messengers of punishment.
The men of Sodom were smitten with blindness by
angels for insulting Lot. The cities of the plain
were destroyed by avenging angels (Gen. 19:11-
13). Judea, under David, was afflicted with a three
days' pestilence by an angel (II Sam. 24:15, 16).
But holy angels punish apart from all malice. They
may even experience much sorrow at the necessity
for thus executing judgment. They share their divine Ruler's pity and regret, who checked the plague
when the beloved city of Jerusalem was so closely
imperiled; and who repented, and turned away from
His fierce anger when He beheld the whole city of
Nineveh prostrate in humiliation (Jonah 3:10).

On the contrary, evil angels experience malevo-
lent pleasure when they can afflict men with disease
or distress. So Satan gloated over Job's calamities.
They love obscurity because their deeds are evil;
and take pains to mystify their methods of operation.
They oppose good angels in their ministrations to
men. Hence the work of the holy angels is often
arduous and difficult. For three full weeks an evil
spirit resisted the great Gabriel, sent forth with a
message of consolation and instruction to the prophet
Daniel. And all that while the beloved Jewish
seer was suffering intense agony, through fasting,
through deferred hope, and through grief at God's

seeming forgetfulness of His covenant Israel. We never should have apprehended how desperate was that mighty conflict over the chosen nation had not the Spirit of God graciously granted us one brief glance behind the veil, and revealed Michael, dispatched from the presence of God to relieve and release his fellow angel from that persistent power of darkness, the evil angel of Persia (Dan. 9:13, 20).

In this connection there may be a deeper meaning than is usually discerned in those words of Paul to Timothy: "In a great house there are not only vessels of gold and of silver, but also of wood and of earth; and some to honor, and some to dishonor." The apostate angels were once golden vessels fitted unto honor. Now, though cast down to dishonor, as the potter flings from his wheel a misshapen vessel, they are still retained for present degraded uses. The believer, whose exalted destiny is that of being a "chosen vessel" to bear the precious name of Jesus, is exhorted to withhold himself from association with these defiled vessels, that he may be fit for the Master's use (II Tim. 2:20, 21). And then finally in summing up his argument about the elected vessels, Paul exhorts Timothy to instruct them in truth, "that they may recover themselves out of the snare of the devil, who are taken captive by him at his will" (II Tim. 2:26).

Because like as the little bird or small animal, charmed by a serpent, lies hypnotized and helpless when a deliverer rescues it, so had some of Christ's weak ones been overpowered by the seductions of

Satan, and now needed to be aroused by the servant of the Lord, that henceforth instead of the Devil's deceptions, they should be brought into willing and wide-awake "captivity to the obedience of Christ" (II Cor. 10:5).

11

SEVEN FORMS OF DEMON PRACTICE

Still following out the investigation of Satan's methods with the ungodly world, we find that seven forms of demonology are recognized and dealt with in the Word of God. These are: *divination, necromancy, prognostication, magic, sorcery, witchcraft, ventriloquism.*

Each of these phases of demonology was in common vogue among the heathen nations; and was each specifically forbidden to Israel, the chosen people of God.

The practice of idolatry always involved one or more of these features of demonology. Thus nature worship of sun, moon, stars, or fire was connected with astrology; while image and hero worship was related to necromancy.

1. *Divination,* briefly defined, was the employment of tokens to indicate good or evil luck. Thus in the case of Jacob, who set peeled and parti-colored rods before his flocks, the idea was borrowed

82

from a superstitious device to which the heathen resorted (Hos. 4:12), though Jacob's inward thought may have been more enlightened than theirs. We do know that in his case the God of Abraham and Isaac overruled the mistakes of His covenant child for the fulfillment of His own purposes of blessings (Gen. 30:38, 39).

His Uncle Laban practiced divination, for he said concerning the teraphim Rachel stole from him: "I have learned by experience"; that is, "I have learned by divination," or "I have hissed, having divined by omens from serpents" (Gen. 30:27).

Joseph's cup in Benjamin's sack furnishes another example. The cup was a very common instrument of divination. We can hardly suppose that so spiritual a worshiper as Joseph would have indulged in this superstition. It rather would seem that he only availed himself of the common belief of his time to carry out his retributive designs toward his guilty brethren (Gen. 44:5).

Divination might be by water, air, fire, earth, the flight of birds, wands, or dreams. God strenuously legislated against it. He commanded those to be stoned who claimed to have a spirit of divination (Lev. 20:27). The reasons for such severe restrictions is plainly made bare. All who sought witchcraft in any form departed from the one true God, and participated in demonology (Lev. 19:31). The same awful principle holds true today. The ages have not changed the character of this false religion. On Scripture authority we assert that whoever consults the occult for guidance and counsel, whether it be by clairvoyance, seance, Mahatma, or some grosser method of spiritualistic communication, is making himself a partner of demonology, and doing it at the eternal peril of his soul.

2. *Necromancy.* This term is from *nekros,* a dead body, and *manteia,* divination. For an example, we have the circumstance of Saul, who specified unto the witch of Endor exactly what he wished her to do. He said: "I pray thee, divine unto me by the familiar spirit, and bring me him up, whom I shall name unto thee" (I Sam. 28:8). Later, in the history of Israel, is the case of King Manasseh, who was what would be called in modern parlance, a "confirmed spiritualist." He is charged with being an observer of times; of using enchantments and witchcraft; of dealing with a familiar spirit and with wizards. It is said, "He wrought much evil in the sight of the Lord, to provoke him to anger." Thus we learn beyond a doubt, how the Lord regards all forms of consultation with spirits. It is heinous sin (II Chron. 33:6).

3. *Prognostication.* This was foretelling the future by means of arrows. They were either shot at a given point, or thrown up in bundles, to see which way they would alight. The king of Babylon supplies an instance of this kind of occult credulity. "He stood at the parting of the way, at the head of the two ways, to use divination: he made his arrows bright [he 'shook' them till they glittered], he consulted with images [teraphim], he looked

in the liver" (Ezek. 21:21). Prognostication thus included the consultation of oracles, and inspection of the entrails of fowls and animals. If these were healthy, they indicated success; if otherwise, failure. Plutarch records the amazing circumstance, yet indicative of the hold superstition has ever had on the heathen and pagan world, that Caesar, just previous to his assassination, ordered many beasts to be sacrificed and inspected in his behalf; and that the augurers failed to find a heart in any of them; which occasioned Shakespeare to make Caesar say:

> Caesar should be a beast without a heart,
> If he should stay at home for fear.

4. *Magic.* The magicians of Egypt were educated priests, and a very important class in the court of the Pharaohs (Gen. 41:8). They were devoted to astronomy, astrology, horoscopy and hierography. They were of a much higher grade than the ordinary demonologist, being in fact scientists. Daniel was, for his superior learning, made president of Nebuchadnezzar's college of wise men. Yet that he never was in collusion with demonology we know from the public prejudice against him concerning his religion (Dan. 6:5). The queen-mother of Belshazzar formed a true estimate of Daniel's exalted wisdom. She said: "There is a man in thy kingdom in whom is the spirit of the holy gods." Jannes and Jambres, who withstood Moses, were of the same class of sacred scribes as Nebuchadnezzar's wise men (Exod. 7:11).

A word of caution to the Christian reader may not be amiss just here. Scientific men are in the present time investigating the supernatural. They are eliminating by their diagnosis all the objectionable superstitions of past dark ages. They claim to be giving to the public innocent occultism. Hypnotism and mind cure and fortune telling are applied to the most beneficent uses. Let us beware. God has set a danger line. We may pass beyond it. And let us confront the fact that great complexity, great obscurity and great plausibility accompany all such forms of revelation. God save all Christians from meddling with what he has prohibited, or from seeking bodily healing in any mysterious or illegitimate way!

5. *Sorcery.* The word means divining by lots. The term implies some art more dishonorable than is conveyed in the practice of magic. For the magicians dealt with the subtle and powerful forces of nature. Astronomy and chemistry formed the basis of their enchantments. They were in possession of many marvelous secrets of nature, which they utilized to stimulate a wondering confidence in themselves. But the sorcerers muttered deceptive and bewildering formula (Isa. 47:9-13). They are called those who peep in the dark. They were far from being altogether impostors; plainly themselves were acted upon by a power beyond their control. There is strong evidence to show that when such believed in the Gospel of Christ, and renounced their deeds of wickedness, they lost their former ability to work

enchantments. Reliable missionaries have reported remarkable instances to this effect among converts to Christianity.[1]

The case recorded in Acts 19:18, 19 is to the point. Pricked in their consciences through the preaching of Paul at Ephesus, "Many that believed came, and confessed, and showed their deeds. Many of them also which used curious arts [the word means labored, overdone incantations], brought their books together [which contained magic characters and receipts], and burned them before all men; and they counted the price of them, and found it fifty thousand pieces of silver" (about $10,000).

There seems, however, to be sufficient reason for charging Simon Magus with imposture. His audacious and profane proposals to purchase the "gift of the Holy Ghost" indicate ignorance of the divine afflatus. Any real vassal of the Devil would have better comprehended his own rank as the leagued instrument of demons. Another statement about him stamps him as fraudulent. It is said in the record that he gave "out that himself was some great one." Thus he industriously published flattering accounts of his achievements to catch public patronage (Acts 8:9-12, 18-20).

In the New Testament, sorcerers are classed among high criminals, to have part in the lake of fire (Rev. 22:15).

6. *Witchcraft.* This designated a compact with

[1]*Demon Possession,* by Dr. Nevius, out of print. Securable second hand only.

the occult, which inferred adoration on the part of the wizard or witch, and patronage and help on the part of the demon. It was a deep, awful, and enslaving art. Astrology might be a science; sorcery a profession or pastime; witchcraft was nothing short of submission to, and conscious complicity with, evil spirits. The term *witchcraft* is not found in the Gospels, though cases of possession are frequently mentioned. Paul gives the sin of witchcraft high rank in his Epistles, and makes it only second to idolatry (Gal. 5:20). While witchcraft was in some respects similar to necromancy, it was in God's sight a more heinous form of demonology. It not simply evoked the spirits of the dead, but it owned and appealed to a ruling power alien to God. Thus it was essentially Devil worship. Hence, the Old Testament counts it rebellion (I Sam. 15:23).

Saul long and strenuously opposed witchcraft in Israel, until the Spirit of God departed from him for other reasons, and an evil spirit took possession of him. Then he resorted to patronage of the same black traffic he had once so vigorously suppressed. Therefore it is recorded: "So Saul died for his transgression [his shuffling evasion of obedience] . . . and also for asking counsel of one that had a familiar spirit, to inquire of it" (I Chron. 10:13).

With such awful words of the living God before us, spoken for universal admonition, how dare any professed Christian so madly apostatize from the right way as to attend the seances of modern spiritualism, or in any other manner lend his encouragement to that wickedness which God abhors so greatly? For spiritualism, in the face of the fact that God declares the canon of divine revelation to be closed (Rev. 22:19), and cursed shall that man be who adds to it—yet spiritualism boldly dares present us with a "new revelation"; and loftily assumes to unfold a "new religion." Giving the lie to David's inspired words about his dead child, "I shall go to him, but he shall not return to me" (II Sam. 12:23), spiritualism teaches that the dead do come back, and David was profoundly mistaken. What further evidence of its blasphemy do Christians need? Automatic writing, which seems so innocent a diversion, has in many instances proved the entering wedge by which witchcraft finally obtained complete domination of the victim.

That spiritualism is to make tremendous progress in the last days is no secret. The New Testament apostles were inspired to foretell its course and development. Thus its present popularity, so far from commending it to our patronage, labels it as infamous, and discounted by God as the way of the thief and robber into His kingdom.

7. *Ventriloquism.* This, primarily, was the utterance of deep, low sounds, through muscular control of the organs of speech. Its method was harmless legerdemain. Its motive was pretension that the voice came from the underground region of the dead. Isaiah describes ventriloquists as those that "peep and mutter" (Isa. 8:19). The Pythoness who followed after Paul and Silas was thus endowed

(Acts 16:17). Job's friend shows his acquaintance with the practice of ventriloquism. Alluding to the inflation which accompanied the indwelling of a familiar spirit, Elihu says: "Behold, my belly is as wine which hath no vent; it is ready to burst like new bottles" (Job 32:19).

In his case it was a mere orientalism of speech; for we nowhere else have it intimated that the true spirit of prophecy was accompanied by unnatural contortions or distensions of the body. Daniel, Isaiah, Ezekiel, John lead us to understand that they were in transport and rapture, but never in agony as they received the living oracles of God. On the contrary, frightful distortion, frenzy, suffering, or collapse to some extent always accompanies the pretended revelations of demons.

Thus it is quite plain that the practice of demonology was something more than juggling trickery or diseased fancy, fascinating weak women and frightening little children, but unworthy the credence of the sturdy minded.

Yet it is probable there is no art in the world that admits of such extensive adulteration with fraud as does the practice of demonology. Hypnotism or clairvoyance, thought-transference, and sleight-of-hand tricks are gladly welcomed as handmaidens to real devilism. The more mystery and complexity, the better for Satan. Four tests will always discover these infernal traffickers. (1) They operate in darkness. (2) They deny the personality of Satan as an evil being. (3) They hate the name of the Lord Jesus. (4) They cast contempt upon the doctrine of the inspiration of the Bible.

Could we but for a brief moment put ourselves upon that vantage ground from which Jehovah looked down upon the inhabitants of this world, we should behold what He saw: all the nations of the earth, save His chosen Israel, gone willingly after idolatry, deceit, and lies; changing the glory of the incorruptible God into images of detestable things, worshiping the creature rather than the Creator, and seeking counsel from the darkness of Hades.

Thus it was, because of the abominable uselessness of idolatry, and all its accessories, that Jehovah fenced in Israel with warnings and prohibitions concerning witchcraft. But they would not be restrained. As early in their national history as at Baal-peor they "sacrificed unto the dead," and "kindled the anger of the Lord" (Ps. 106:28, 29). Under their first king, because of his necromancy, the kingdom was rent from him (I Sam. 28:17).

Two eternal monuments, lighthouses of warning planted on the coast of the ages, remain to testify to God's wrath—Balaam is one; a man among the prophets, attempting to combine soothsaying with holy prophecy. Judas is the other; a man among the apostles, feigning to follow the Son of God, while he himself was the son of perdition. Their judgment proclaims that it is damnation to make "godliness a source of gain"; since there can be no enchantment against Jacob, neither divination against Israel, that shall not perish in the "raging waves of the sea of blackness of darkness forever" (Num. 23:23; Jude 11-13).

Thus divination by unseen agents and through familiar spirits was denounced very early in unsparing terms in Mosaic law. "Thou shalt not suffer a witch to live" (Exod. 22:18).

"The soul that turneth after such as have familiar spirits, and after wizards, to go a whoring after them, I will even set my face against that soul, and will cut him off from among his people" (Lev. 20:6).

"There shall not be found among you any one that maketh his son or his daughter to pass through the fire, or that useth divination, or an observer of times, or an enchanter, or a witch, or a charmer, or a consulter with familiar spirits, or a wizard, or a necromancer. For all that do these things are an abomination unto the Lord" (Deut. 18:10-12).

The Bible shows clearly that the dead do not return or communicate with man (Eccles. 9:5, 6; II Sam. 12:23; Luke 16:26). Hence, Scripture recognizes Satan and his demons as the real speakers in these communications. The witch of Endor was the mistress of a spirit (I Sam. 28:7). She was not a mere trickster, but a genuine spiritualist. When Samuel appeared, she cried out in fright, for she had never seen the like before. She also immediately recognized Saul under his disguise. The whole affair was extraordinary, and exceeded even the wonders of demonology. God took the case into His own hands. He answered Saul according to his folly

(Ezek. 14:4, 7, 8). Samuel in this exceptional case was seen and delivered a true and awful prophecy. Both Saul and the woman who herself had long been accustomed to intercourse with the occult realized this manifestation as divine, and they were appalled and distressed with sufficient reason.

Apart from the degrading moral effects of partnership with evil spirits, God forbade the traffic on theocratic grounds. There was but one God; one divine Spirit; one authoritative channel of revelation. The whole compact of demonology, in all its complex manifestations of idolatry or enchantment, was arrayed against the supreme and wholesome rule of the heavens. It taught falsehood; it acted lies; it inculcated deceit; it discouraged purity; it gloated over foulness; it shunned the light; it operated in the darkness; it never healed, but always hurt; it plagued the bodies, and damned the souls of men; it multiplied violence in the earth; it invented supernatural schemes of torment; it drove men into dungeons to feed on the bread and water of affliction; it cut them with knives and wounded them with stones; it frenzied women, and thrust little children into the arms of fire; it made fools of kings, and demons of queens; it defiled the beautiful temple of God and desecrated the oracle of Jehovah; it ascended to the heights of the clouds, and descended to the depths of Hell in the sweep of its tremendous effects. Its standing monuments are such monstrous characters as the Nephilim of the

Deluge; the builders of Babel; the Pharaohs of
Egypt; the giants of Anak; the kings of Babylon;
as Balaam, as Saul, as Jezebel, as Ahaz, as Antiochus,
as Simon Magus, as Elymas, as the false prophet
of the Apocalypse.

12

SATANIC MODES WITH THE CHURCH

We are now to investigate the methods of demons with the Church of God. In the hearts of the unregenerate, Satan encounters no rival power. Such are "of the world," and not of Christ. They are wholly carnal; that is, "in the flesh." By nature they lie under the power of that wicked one who is still permitted to be "the god of this world," a world ruler, but not a universe ruler.

In relation to the Church of Christ, this condition of things has been entirely changed. The Christian has been called out from the world and the dominion of Satan to become identified with the Lord Jesus. A new and holy power indwells and controls all such. And this divine Spirit of God, resident in the believer, antagonizes and contests the influences of the Devil. Hence, we read of the warfare of Christian life, ever wrestling against the powers of darkness; and of mysterious victories gained over the world, the flesh, and the Devil, "through the blood of the Lamb." Such experiences are riddles to the unconverted. They never have them while lying quiescent in the captivity of Satan. They are only known when a soul arises from the stupor of sin and endeavors to shake off its fetters of thraldom and transfer its allegiance to God.

Because of this decisive change which faith in Christ produces in the soul, we read in the New Testament of Satan's fourfold and distinctive procedure with Christians: (1) His designs (II Cor. 2:11). (2) His stratagems (Eph. 6:11, 12). (3) His snares (I Tim. 3:7). (4) His lying wonders (II Thess. 2:9).

And we find, as we come to examine New Testament evidence on demonology, that those descriptive terms which abound in the Old Testament are exchanged for other phraseology. The cruder forms of superstition are no longer dealt with. The apostles present Satan as a more subtle foe than did ever the inspired prophets. Great power characterizes him in the Old Testament, but great craftiness distinguishes him in the New Testament. It requires his most adroit deceptions to delude those who are enlightened by the Spirit of God.

Hence, we are informed that he quotes Scripture (Matt. 4:6); transforms himself into an angel of light (II Cor. 11:14); afflicts the body (II Cor. 12:7); causes weakness that paralyzes Christian activity (I Cor. 5:5); picks away the seed of the Word (Mark 4:15); sows harmful tares (Matt. 13:38, 39); he thrusts in impure thoughts (I Cor.

7:0); he specially tempts by pride (I Tim. 3:6); he uses outward circumstances to hinder (I Thess. 2:18); he causes evil men to pervert the Gospel of Christ (Acts 13:10); he seduces some from Christ by pleasure (I Tim. 5:11, 15); he seeks to intimidate others by persecution (Rev. 2:10); he sifts some quickly, like Peter (Luke 22:31); he oppresses others for long periods, like the bent woman with the spirit of infirmity (Luke 13:16); he buffeted Paul (II Cor. 12:7); he made shipwreck of Hymenaeus and Alexander (I Tim. 1:19, 20); he tempted Ananias to hypocrisy, and Sapphira to lying (Acts 5:3); he certainly made one apostate—Judas (John 13:27); and Scripture warns us that others shall forsake the truth; for "the Spirit speaketh expressly, that in the latter times some shall depart from the faith, giving heed to seducing spirits, and doctrines of demons" (I Tim. 4:1).

The three cases of the exorcists; the seven sons of Sceva; and the magicians of Ephesus (all mentioned in Acts 19) give a good impression of how prevalent and recognized an evil was demonology in the early age of the Church. So common were *damonia* that the profession of exorcism found abundant opportunity for flourishing. *Exorcism*, a word from the Greek which means to conjure, was the practice of expelling demons by the use of the name of God. The terms *exorcism* and *conjuring* were then synonymous. Some modifications subsequently became attached to the words. We now understand an exorcist to be one who drives away evil spirits; while a conjurer is one who calls them up.

We stated that Jewish exorcists expelled demons through repetition of the supreme name. With this idea in mind, of special potency in some name, we shall better understand the force of such language as that which Peter used to the lame man: "In the name of Jesus Christ of Nazareth rise up and walk." And further, when explaining the miracle, he declared: "His name through faith in his name, hath made this man strong" (Acts 3:6, 16). Such formula, of conjuring through some potent name, being perfectly familiar to both Jewish and heathen ears, Peter used it with the direct intention of magnifying the superhuman power of the despised Nazarene.

And further, it is plain that this power of exorcism did legitimately exist in our Lord's lifetime. He made recognition of the fact when He said to the caviling Jews: "If I by Beelzebub cast out devils, by whom do your children cast them out?" (Matt. 12:27). So the apostles talked confidentially with their Lord as over a common event: "Master, we saw one casting out devils in thy name; and we forbade him, because he followeth not with us. And Jesus said unto them, Forbid him not: for he that is not against us is for us" (Luke 9:49, 50). We also understand from two other records in the Gospels, that this power was specially bestowed by Christ himself upon His disciples: "These signs shall follow them that believe. In my name shall they cast out devils" (Mark 16:17).

The specifications in the heavenly charter are deeply interesting: "I give unto you power to tread on serpents and scorpions, and over all the power of the enemy: and nothing shall by any means hurt you" (Luke 10:19). A serpent and a scorpion we might well suppose would be among the most infrequent of the perils that a missionary would encounter in preaching the Gospel. Why should Jesus enumerate these and omit other dangers that would certainly be more common and disastrous? Notice! He connects them with "the power of the enemy"; and this furnishes the clue. Serpents have ever constituted a prime agency in demonology. In this guise Satan first appeared to man. Under this form he has been perpetually worshiped and dreaded.

Christianity was sent forth to match and enter combat with demonology. Literal serpents, as in the case of Moses before Pharaoh, would be used to counterfeit the miracles wrought in the power of the divine Christ. These the disciples might have occasion to handle, or might be stung by. Hence our Lord promised they should be innocuous to their deadly influences. That the promise was in due time realized, one record confirms. Paul shook a poisonous viper from his hand unharmed; and to the barbarous people of Melita it was proof conclusive that the apostle possessed supernatural endowments (Acts 28:3-6).

From the first, demons dreaded the exorcism of Christians. The Early Church so thoroughly recognized exorcism that they practiced it over catechumens before they were admitted to the privileges of baptism and communion, keeping all suspected ones in separation till there was full proof of their restoration.

It is unreasonable, therefore, for scientific and medical men to assert, as some do, that demonology is the mere figment of a diseased sensibility or a magnetized brain. The Bible throughout affirms the collusion of men and demons. Our Lord made provision for His Church in future contact with them. The apostles and early teachers legislated concerning them. To deny the activity of demons is to insult the Inspirer of Holy Scripture.

The history of the seven sons of Sceva is one of great value as proof of these statements. In this narrative the afflicted man is carefully distinguished from the evil spirit who obsessed him. The demon made the man so strong that he fought and mastered the exorcists. The confession of this impure spirit is very notable as an exhibition of infernal wisdom as well as power. Two words are used in the original, both translated *know*, to express this spirit's understanding. With singular discrimination, he cried out: "Jesus I know [I recognize or discern], and Paul I know [I am acquainted with]; but who are ye?" It was a taunting way of asserting, You are impostors for whom I have no respect (Acts 19:13-17).

There seems to be good evidence for believing that during Christ's presence in the earth demoniacal manifestations were greatly intensified. He had come as the Son of God, the heir of all things. Messengers, servants, prophets, priests had been sent before. All these had been shamefully treated and disbelieved. God said: "They will reverence my son"; so he sent Him (Mark 12:1-7). Never before had One of absolute purity been thus incarnate on earth. Never before had One dwelt among men in whom Satan could find none occasion for accusation. Never before had One appeared with the direct commission "to destroy the works of the devil." Angels had often descended and done great and glorious work for distressed humanity. But not one of these had come to wrest the government of this world from Satan's grasp, and "destroy [or bring to nought] him that had the power of death, that is, the devil; and deliver them who through fear of death were all their lifetime subject to bondage" (Heb. 2:14, 15).

The legions of Satan knew the divine Man, and they dreaded Him. Himself they dared not assault; so their malice, envenomed by the consciousness of approaching and final defeat, vented itself on such victims as they could control. It rather would seem that the demons then believed and expected what would have transpired had not the Jews blindly rejected their "time of visitation"; namely, the immediate establishment of God's royal kingdom in the earth, with His Son upon the throne of David, and the heathen and the uttermost parts of the earth given Him for an everlasting possession (Luke 19:

38, 42-44). All their confessions, whenever rebuked by Christ, prove this.

We never read of any demon underestimating the dignity and authority of Jesus Christ. They believed, though they trembled at His presence (James 2:19). One said: "Art thou come to destroy us? I know thee, who thou art, the Holy One of God" (Mark 1:24). This acknowledgment is very remarkable. The superior wisdom of the demons gave them such unerring apprehension as none of the priests or rulers possessed. We may well raise the question: Why should Satan have allowed his hosts to witness such damaging confessions? Jesus found it necessary, as in the case of the possessed man in the synagogue of Capernaum (Luke 4:34, 35), to silence the ever-too-ready testimony of those impure spirits. Their fulsome acknowledgments complicated and compromised His own testimony, making Him seem to be in collusion with the demons, which was precisely what His enemies were anxious to assert of Him.

13

DELUSIONS AT THE CLOSE OF THIS AGE

A s it was at the first coming of the Lord, so we are authorized to expect it will be shortly previous to His second coming, when He shall return to assume the kingly rule suspended for nineteen centuries through Jewish unbelief. The demons are to understand the times, for Paul says that "the Spirit speaketh expressly, that in the latter times some shall . . . giving heed to . . . doctrines of devils" (I Tim. 4:1). Other Scriptures inform us that just before the advent, sorcery, spiritualism, and various lying anti-Christian wonders shall prevail (II Thess. 2:9, 10; II Tim. 3:1, 6, 8; Rev. 13:13, 14; 16:13, 14). Satan understood Old Testament Scripture, and quoted it readily. There is no reason to doubt his understanding New Testament Scripture as well, and from it the divine plan of the dispensations. As his time shortens, and his overthrow approaches, his wrath will increase and his deceptions multiply.

We have no assurance from the Word that we

are, at the close of this age, to look for such purely physical forms of demoniacal manifestation as were encountered at the first advent. But rather, principally, the Devil shall conform himself to modern widespread conditions of Christian knowledge and civilization, and act the great role of "an angel of light." The study of all mysteries pertaining to the "Borderland" will become a fad of the last days. And Satan well knows how to forge a chain of links which shall include mythology, psychology, theosophy, mesmeric healing, necromancy, and so on, through all the varied fields of occult science up to avowed and blasphemous Devil worship.

We are to see demon power put forth in multitudinous forms of false religions and distorted ethics. Crooked thinking will produce unrighteous acting. Suicide, murder, and impurity will be crystallized into heroic virtues. We are sustained in such statements by the present general trend of common sentiment. Popular magazines are devoted to matter pertaining to the occult and weird. It is what the public taste demands. We have grown tired of the old-fashioned, fictitious love story. We crave the eccentric, the mysterious, and the devilish.

The Bible further indicates that amid all the complex mixture of good and evil which the Devil shall produce, one prominent feature will be seen: Men and women shall be strongly religious while utterly godless. Amid the practice of the wildest fanaticism or the most open iniquity, they shall fancy themselves pursuing an ideal of supreme truth. The

Scriptures, which it would be impracticable and impossible for Satan to totally *deny*, he will make to serve more effective and mischievous purpose by *misinterpreting.*

Christian metaphysics, so-called, is proof of this. Scripture is acknowledged, but frightfully distorted. Ancient landmarks of doctrine are removed, and the Bible made to teach things the fathers never dreamed of.

We might add further that modern spiritualism, which openly claims to be necromancy, is now at this present time by its teachings and practices furnishing exact earnests of this future universal condition of things. There is not a villainy or indecency the Devil has ever produced that may not today somewhere among the ranks of spiritualists find its warm promoters.

All these satanic disguises, let it be remembered, pertain to Christendom, where the knowledge of Christ has been disseminated if not individually embraced. With the heathen the Devil has no need for stratagems. Where the light of the Gospel has not dispelled the ignorance of nature's darkness, his sway is easy and unhindered.

Yet no believer need of necessity yield to his heretic influences. The "strong man armed" has met a "stronger than he" who has spoiled his goods (Luke 11:20-22). Jesus has ascended up on high, leading captivity captive (Eph. 4:8). "Having spoiled principalities and powers, he made a show of them openly, triumphing over them in it" (Col.

2:15). There is a very pertinent promise recorded to encourage the saints in their conflict with the powers of darkness: "God is faithful, who will not suffer you to be tempted above that ye are able; but will with the temptation make also the way of escape, that ye may be able to bear it" (I Cor. 10:13).

Simply and comprehensively has the Bible marked out the plan for Christian conduct in reference to the Devil.

1. We are warned to beware of him as the devouring lion (I Peter 5:8).

2. We are commanded to resist him as the tempter to pride (James 4:7).

3. We are forbidden to hold any parley with him as the provoker to wrath (Eph. 4:27).

4. We are instructed to fight him with truth as the foe to righteousness (Eph. 6:17).

5. We are promised he shall not touch us as the Evil One (I John 5:18).

If we are not watchful, and do suffer ourselves to be "taken captive of the devil at his will," the Holy Spirit, God's judicial keeper of the saints, holds power to deliver us over "for the destruction of the flesh, that the spirit may be saved in the day of the Lord Jesus" (I Cor. 5:5; I Tim. 1:20). Such was the case with Hymenaeus, Alexander, and some Corinthian believers (I Cor. 5:5; I Tim. 1:20).

No words of the Epistles are more mysterious and awful than these. It is the case of a child of God, once made free through the truth, and for some time walking in the life and light of the Gospel. Having lapsed, he is, by the edict of his heavenly Father, delivered back to the bondage of Satan, afflicted in his body, made weak and morally helpless, for the possible recovery of the spirit from eternal condemnation. The heart shudders at the personal possibility of any of us coming under such chastening; and the awakened conscience cries out, "Lord, is it I?"

Does not the experience of King Saul furnish a forecast of this condition of some in the Church? Because Saul rejected the <u>Word</u> of the Lord, the Spirit of the Lord departed from him, and an evil spirit from God terrified him (I Sam. 16:14).

We are happy, however, to state our conviction that under the present dispensation of the Spirit, experiences similar to that of Saul must be exceptional. Before Pentecost the Spirit abode transiently in the world, identifying himself with offices rather than with persons. Since Pentecost his "abiding" in the church is a pledge for her preservation from the Evil One.

Our Lord endured extreme temptations from Satan that He might have partnership in every delusion and affliction that fallen mankind has inherited from its first deceived ancestors. We are told He was in all points tempted like as we, and "in that he himself hath suffered being tempted, he is able to succor them that are tempted" (Heb. 4:15; 2:18). Never, except on that unparalleled occasion, was the Devil permitted, undisguised and persistently, thus to approach any human being.

Nor could mere human nature have sustained such trial of soul, body, and spirit. Nothing so morally magnificent has ever transpired on earth; perhaps nothing so grand and pathetic in all the universe.

We have a tolerably full record of those three mysterious temptations, which appear to have followed each other in near succession, at the close of the forty days, when the Lord was exhausted from long exposure and weak from want of food. But of the profound secrets of that whole forty days, during which Satan appears never to have left the Saviour, or ceased his infernal vexations, we know nothing. Eternal counsels have locked up those scenes of conflict beyond the prying scrutiny of human eyes. Doubtless flesh and blood could not endure to hear of what God knows, and what angels saw, when He, the Son of God, as Son of man, undertook to overthrow the works of the Devil.

One other subsequent encounter is recorded. It is the fight of the cross. Our Lord goes with strong assurance to this final conflict. Through death He is to "destroy him that had the power of death." We hear him courageously say: "The prince of this world cometh, and hath nothing in me." He is troubled in spirit, but not for Himself; it is for others; for Peter, and for any of His redeemed flock who should in aftertime deny Him and crucify unto themselves the Son of God afresh. He sweats great drops of blood; but that is not from dread of Satan; it is because the Lord Jehovah is about to "lay on him the iniquity of us all." Griefs, high as mountains and deep as seas, are pressing Him from above and submerging Him beneath. Curses, swift and terrible as thunderbolts, are falling on Him. The bread corn for the world is to be ground between the upper and the nether millstone of divine wrath. The darkness of death and the yawning abyss of Hell are ready to engulf Him. Even Satan, the arch-author of all this woe, becomes himself but a pigmy now in the overwhelming presence of this progeny of giants, this great army which he has begotten of iniquities, transgressions, and sin, to purge the universe from which the Son of man is about to lay down His life.

14

THE FINAL DOOM OF DEMONS

Closely following upon the first temptation, Scripture proclaims the downfall of Satan's kingdom and the method of its accomplishment. "I will put enmity between thee and the woman, and between thy seed and her seed; it shall bruise thy head and thou shalt bruise his heel" (Gen. 3:15). There can be little question, however, that sometime previous to this God had pronounced sentence on the apostate angels for other crimes. Peter affirms: "God spared not the angels that sinned, but cast them down to hell, and delivered them into chains of darkness, to be reserved unto judgment" (II Peter 2:4). Of their destiny they appear to be clearly cognizant. They also seem to know, at least approximately, how long respite is allowed them. It is satirically sad to read of their crying out to the Son of God, "Art thou come hither to torment us before the time?" (Matt. 8:29). With a pretentious sense of justice, they demand that the supreme Judge shall not antedate the appointed time of their punishment.

Some of the earliest Christians held the view that the redeemed were elected to fill up the vacant places in the heavenly spheres made through the fall and removal of apostate angels. While this idea may not militate against general Scripture teaching, it certainly trenches upon secrets in the heavenly counsels, with which we have no right to meddle. Redeemed souls, by virtue of their union with the Son of God, are to take precedence above angels in the ages to come. It is stated in Luke 20:36, that in their resurrection state the saints shall be "equal unto the angels." But that word *equal* refers not to grade or rank, but designates the deathless condition which shall then be common both to angels and to glorified men.

Why the angels were permitted to sin, and forsake their own proper government, we do not know. In Revelation 10:7, the overthrow of Satan is called "the finishing of the mystery of God." That statement runs parallel with Revelation 20:7-11, where the extreme end of the penalty is executed upon the Devil. John was told to seal up the voices of the seven thunders; and until God's great phonograph shall be opened, no human prophecy can liberate the import of those things uttered. Thus the obscurities which attend the existence of demons throughout deepen and multiply as we advance toward the end of their career.

It is evident there are appointed two stages in the

judgment of demons; and these are separated by the vast interval of one thousand years. During this period the powers of evil shall be bound, and the Millennium of peace, holiness, and divine manifestation shall be running its course upon the earth.

Might we venture for one moment to indulge in fancy, we can imagine with what baffled rage *Diabolos* and his demons, foiled in every endeavor to overthrow the kingdom of Christ, shall then grind in helplessness, while continually cognizant of the holy pleasures and high honors, unmarred by their malicious hands, which the transfigured saints and purified nations are enjoying throughout those blessed cycles of triumphant grace and defeated sin.

The two stages in the Devil's downfall reveal two places of punishment: the bottomless pit and the lake of fire. It is not easy to discover what are the essential differences between that house of detention and that final prison. We are not told that the Devil is tormented with fire while in the abyss; we are informed he shall be in the lake of burning. That he does not go to the bottomless pit alone, but is accompanied by his legions, two Scriptures show. When Jesus was about to cast out the multitude of demons from the man in the tombs, "they entreated him that he would not command them to depart into the abyss" (Luke 8:31, R. V.). Again, in the Apocalypse (Rev. 9), clothed in vivid imagery, are seen the hosts of Satan in association, mobilized for war. The bottomless pit is opened, and therefrom emerges a great army of terrible locusts, having power to torment as scorpions; the very creatures, be it remembered, over which Jesus had given power in His commission to the first disciples (Luke 10:19).

If we cannot determine to what extent the description of these locusts may be literal or symbolic, let us reverently bear in mind one fact—a symbol is always less than the idea symbolized. Falsehood may exaggerate. Truth never does. Circumstances far more dreadful than the sting of envenomed scorpions, or the rage of hungry lions, or the horrors of war, are here depicted for our consideration.

These locusts "had a king over them, the angel of the abyss: his name in Hebrew is Abaddon, and in the Greek tongue he hath his name Apollyon." Their identity as demons is thus established. They have power to materialize after the hideous fashion described. As in their handling of Job, they have authority to hurt and annoy, but not to kill. Since they are as invincible as hyacinth-stone, no arts of war can destroy them.

Joel, occupied more with their deeds than their appearance, seems to describe them in his prophecy. It is noticeable he does not say these strange warriors are men, but they "run like mighty men."

"The appearance of them is as the appearance of horses; and as horsemen, so shall they run. Like the noise of chariots on the tops of mountains shall they leap, like the noise of a flame of fire that devoureth the stubble, as a strong people set in battle array. Before their face the people shall be much pained: all faces shall gather blackness. They shall run like mighty men; they shall climb the wall like men of war; and they shall march every one on his ways, and they shall not break their ranks: neither shall one thrust another; they shall walk every one in his path: and when they fall upon the sword, they shall not be wounded. They shall run to and fro in the city; they shall run upon the wall, they shall climb up upon the houses; they shall enter in at the windows like a thief. The earth shall quake before them; the heavens shall tremble; the sun and the moon shall be dark; and the stars shall withdraw their shining" (Joel 2:4-10).

St. John's picture of the demons is a combination of the intelligence of man, the subtle perceptions of woman, the gross animal instincts of beasts, the agility of flying creatures, and the sly venom of poisonous reptiles. Their crowns betoken authority; their breath depravity; and their shields supermortality.

"And the shapes of the locusts were like unto horses prepared unto battle; and on their heads were as it were crowns like gold, and their faces were as the faces of men. And they had hair as the hair of women, and their teeth were as the teeth of lions. And they had breastplates, as it were breastplates of iron; and the sound of their wings was as the sound of chariots of many horses running to battle. And they had tails like unto scorpions, and there were stings in their tails: and their power was to hurt men five months. And they had a king over them, which is the angel of the bottomless pit, whose name in the Hebrew tongue is Abaddon, but in the Greek tongue hath his name Apollyon. . . . And the number of the army of the horsemen were two hundred thousand thousand: and I heard the number of them. And thus I saw the horses in the vision, and them that sat on them, having breastplates of fire, and of jacinth, and brimstone: and the heads of the horses were as the heads of lions; and out of their mouths issued fire and smoke and brimstone" (Rev. 9:7-11, 16, 17).

Two very interesting queries arise just here:

1. Who is Abaddon or Apollyon? The Hebrew signifies *perdition;* the Greek, *destroyer.* It is the opinion of many expositors that he is not Satan himself, but the Devil's chief angel. And that when the bottomless pit is opened to loose this king and his hosts, the key is in the hand of the personal Satan, who, as "Lucifer, the star fallen from heaven," shall have this power granted him (Rev. 9:1, 2).

2. How does it happen then that Satan is free and separated from his demons, while they are in the pit? Decision in the matter of Abaddon is of secondary moment. Either view of his identity may be held, and not throw the other general facts in the case out of harmony. But it is highly important to every part of the scene to ascertain who is the pit opener. If Satan himself, as many expositors assert, then but one plausible explanation of his presence under such circumstances can be given.

And this solution, because of Scripture reticence, can only be offered suggestively.

We must suppose these locust-demons represent only a faction of the fallen angels. When the Nephilim sinned, whose crime was so atrocious, they were immediately punished. To this idea agree the words of Peter: "God spared not the angels that sinned, but cast them down to hell [the abyss, or *tartarus*, the Greek term for pit], and delivered them into chains [of dens, as some oldest Manuscripts read] of darkness, to be reserved unto judgment" (II Peter 2:4). That is, they were immediately confined, with a prospect of future severer punishment.

With this thought most singularly harmonizes Jude's statement: "And the angels which kept not their first estate, but left their own habitation, he hath reserved in everlasting chains under darkness unto the judgment of the great day. Even as Sodom and Gomorrah, and the cities about them in like manner, giving themselves over to fornication, and going after strange flesh, are set forth for an example, suffering the vengeance of eternal fire" (Jude 6, 7).

Sodom and Gomorrah are exhibited as their parallel. These cities went after strange flesh, demanding Lot's angel-visitors for carnal abuse. For their awful wickedness they were suddenly overwhelmed with fire. Our Lord represents them as "nevertheless yet waiting for judgment" (Matt. 10:15).

The angels, Jude tells us, sinned "after the same fashion," committing fornication with the daughters of men (Gen. 6:1-5). For their unnatural crime they were speedily committed to "dens of darkness" to await later judgment. There might be myriads of other apostate angels who did not participate in the high sin of these Nephilim. We have ground for thinking so, from the twofold nature of the divine indictment: "They neglected their own proper government; they left their own habitation" (physical tabernacle) All seem to have revolted from the divine government. But all may not have degraded themselves to material forms. These former, having no bodies of their own, have since ever manifested a liking for possessing men's bodies.

If anyone thinks we are putting an exaggerated interpretation upon the record in Genesis in asserting that fallen angels held carnal intercourse with material beings, we reply that modern spiritualism, quite apart from this Scripture narrative, holds to precisely this power on the part of unseen beings. A notable experimenter with the things of the spirit land tells in her biography through her biographer that she had "a curious vision wherein she was surrounded by fascinating male spirits who caressed her body, and promised she should be the most blessed among women if she would exchange earthly love for the delights of affinity with angels." She further tells us she repelled their overtures altogether unprepared for this "new kind of crime, strange and monstrous." We believe this woman had this vision, and that demons were the actors.

We have no right to say she was the victim of a
diseased fancy, or of her own filthy impulses.

But to return to Apollyon. We have glanced at
one phase of this great mystery, logically followed
out. Our own personal impression is that Apollyon
and Satan are identical, he, and he only, standing
as the counterpart of Michael. Assumption has made
him to exceed his own legitimate greatness. We think
that the key of the bottomless pit is given to the
"fifth angel" and not to Satan. It confuses figures
to say a key is given to a star. It is against the whole
tenor of Revelation to put judicial authority into
the hands of any but holy avenging angels. After
the fashion of the Book (Rev. 9), describing the
locusts is one of many concise visions, complete in
itself, and not necessarily following any previous
scenes in chronological order. The "fifth angel" lets
out Apollyon and his demons; as is once more stated
in chapter 20, where the whole tremendous pano-
rama of a thousand years is condensed into one
limited picture, requiring but a few brief sentences
to describe it all. The royal keys of state are never
committed to the hands of thieves and robbers.
Jesus said: "He that hath the key of David, he
that openeth and no man shutteth; and shutteth
and no man openeth" (Rev. 3:7).

15

THE CHURCH TO PARTICIPATE IN THE JUDGMENT OF DEMONS

G OD HAS BEEN PLEASED to appoint the Church to have the peculiar honor of association with Jesus Christ in the judgment upon the powers of evil. Writes Paul, "Know ye not that we shall judge angels?" And again, "The God of peace shall bruise Satan under your feet shortly" (I Cor. 6:3; Rom. 16:20). This we might expect, since it is promised repeatedly that the saints are to have partnership with their Lord in all His future administration of government.

The full execution of the sentence upon these apostates is fixed at the close of that great period known in Scripture as the "day of the Lord." *Tophet, Hell, the pit, everlasting fire,* and similar terms used to indicate the place of torment, are mentioned as prepared expressly for the Devil and his angels, which statement we infer means that even before man was created, and had himself come under sentence of punishment, God had ordained the place of Satan's doom; and that, when man sinned, the same place of everlasting fire was made available for his punishment also.

Isaiah says: "Tophet is ordained of old; yea, for the king it is prepared: he hath made it deep and large: the pile thereof is fire and much wood; the breath of the Lord, like a stream of brimstone, doth kindle it" (Isa. 30:33).

John's words agree with the prophet's: "The devil that deceived them was cast into the lake of fire and brimstone, where the beast and the false prophet are, and shall be tormented day and night forever and ever" (Rev. 20:10).

Our Lord's utterance makes it clear that the demons share a common fate with their prince: "Then shall he [the King] say also unto those on the left hand, Depart from me, ye cursed, into everlasting fire, prepared for the devil and his angels" (Matt. 25:41).

Before they arrive at this final destiny, they are to be allowed participation in some atrocious acts of wickedness. Six thousand years of experience will but have developed their craftiness and intensified their malice. Knowing their time is limited, they compact for one prodigious stroke of iniquity. The manifestation of the last Antichrist, who shall gather unto himself all the features of sin displayed severally by his notable precursors, shall be the Devil's great masterpiece.

Whatever view Bible students take of "the man

of sin," whether it be claimed that the terms designate a malign *personality*, or a stupendous iniquitous *scheme*, all must submit to one Scripture verdict —"the dragon gave him his power, and his seat, and great authority" (Rev. 13:2). All must further admit the Scriptures to say that this iniquitous factor shall be found practicing and prospering "at the time of the end," and shall be miraculously destroyed by the personal and glorious appearance of the Lord Jesus (Dan. 8:24, 25; II Thess. 2:8).

The subject of this treatise, though so closely allied to latter-day evils, does not permit our divergence to discuss peculiar theories of the Antichrist. We must return to him who is the great energizer of the beast power, and in general outlines trace his closing acts.

None can read his Bible aright and not perceive that this dispensation shall wind up with more stupendous manifestations of wickedness, disaster, and miracle than the world has ever seen. What other explanation of the fact can be given than the reason which Scripture asserts? "Woe to the inhabiters of the earth and of the sea! for the devil is come down unto you, having great wrath, because he knoweth that he hath but a short time" (Rev. 12:12).

Throughout his final schemes of iniquity Satan mimics the principles of Deity. There is plainly a masterly attempt to divert attention from the real kingdom of God to the spurious kingdom of the beast. As God has His beloved Son, so Satan has his son of perdition. As God, through His holy child

Jesus, wrought "miracles and wonders and signs" (Acts 4:30-33), so Satan, through the man of sin, works lying wonders, with all deceivableness of unrighteousness. As God commands all to acknowledge His Christ, so Satan shall coerce all, both bond and free, high and low, to worship the beast. The true saints are to wear God's name in their foreheads; the worshipers of the dragon are to be branded with the number of his name. He sets his blood-stained harlot over against the pure Bride of the Lamb. As there is a trinity of holiness, so Satan links himself with the beast and the false prophet to form a trinity of evil. The coincidence of counterfeits can be traced throughout the Book of Revelation, till at last the Great Tribulation ends with this compact of evil disbanded, the beast and false prophet cast into the lake of fire, and the dragon bound and shut up in the abyss for a thousand years.

Hostilities are suspended, and tortured earth finds rest at last. The devastated creation dries her tears, and begins to revive under the soothing influences of righteousness. Thorns give place to flowers, parched wastes to fruitful fields, fierce discords to gentle harmonies. Sickness is the exception, and health the rule; great longevity makes death uncommon; blasphemy is banished, and praise prevails. The heathen cast their idols to the moles and the bats, and God is universally adored. The Sun of Righteousness arises with healing in His wings; the night of sin disappears, and day, beautiful, perfect millennial day, is spread over all the earth.

How far these Scripture suggestions are literal we need not here discuss. Enough for the present purpose to know that the language of prophecy indicates a time of exalted felicity for the earth and the nations, far surpassing anything of the past.

Fain would we now end our investigation, and close this history of the fallen angels. But we must be faithful to all Scripture testimony. Startling words of inspiration confront us here: *"The devil must be loosed a little season."* How amazing! Why this dreadful necessity? The statement is sovereign and absolute. He must be liberated. Divine justice will give to the whole universe one last proof of the undying, irremediable power of sin. A thousand years' imprisonment makes no penitent of Satan or his demons, and works no radical change in those who have not been sealed with the blood of the Lamb (Rev. 20:3, 6).

Ungrateful for his reprieve, and unrepentant for his crimes, no sooner is he at liberty than he begins to plot gigantic mischief. He goes out to deceive the nations which are in the four quarters of the earth, a company as innumerable as the sands of the sea. And now we get a larger view of Satan's character than we have anywhere had before. If by his past deeds he has impressed us, by this one he appalls us. How great indeed must such a creature be who can wield such an influence under such circumstances! Because, let it be carefully marked, for a whole chiliad of time the inhabitants of the world shall have been under the perfectly righteous sway of the Prince of Peace. Conditions the most favorable, prosperous, and holy for man's happiness and growth in goodness shall have continuously prevailed.

And yet—with the odds of such benign influences all against him that great fallen angel shall be able, in an exceedingly brief space of time, to stir up the spirit of disobedience in millions of human beings, and set them in hostile array against the government of the Son of God. It is difficult for the human mind to conceive of such a deed. With some show of right, men and women revolt against that which is imperfect and oppressive in human governments. But throughout the whole code of millennial law, we read of only one coercive restriction: "It shall come to pass, that . . . all the nations . . . shall even go up from year to year to worship the King, the Lord of hosts, and to keep the feast of tabernacles. And it shall be, that whoso will not come up of all the families of the earth unto Jerusalem to worship the King, the Lord of hosts, even upon them shall be no rain. . . . This shall be the punishment . . . of all nations" (Zech. 14:16-19).

Have we not, then, in this marshaling of Gog and Magog, at the muster of Satan, one of the most majestic demonstrations that could possibly be furnished the world of *the implacable and unimprovable quality of sin?* What else could be shown us that would so enhance *the necessity and value of divine atonement?* or so vindicate the righteousness of God *in the everlasting punishment of unforgiven sinners?*

In Eden we get a microscopic view of sin. On the camp of Gog we get a telescopic view. And all the crimes, the woes, the deaths, from Eden to Armageddon (Rev. 16:14-16), are the work of this mighty archfiend through the myriad agencies of his demon messengers. What a stupendous wreck of truth! What a relentless foe of goodness! We wonder at him while we loathe him. We tremble for ourselves while we behold him afar off, lest he deceive us also. We pray as our Lord taught us: "Carry us not over to his temptations, but deliver us from the evil one, for *thine* is the kingdom," and not *his.*

But his end is promised, certain, effectual, and suitable. All divine predictions have a peculiar forward look toward that time when demon assumption shall meet its eternal doom in the lake of fire. In no other light can we interpret the prophetic praises of David; the ecstatic visions of Daniel; the seraphic futures of Isaiah; the glowing mysteries of Ezekiel; the ringing exultation of Habakkuk; the joyful battle cry of Joel; the victorious confidence of the exiled John. To each it had been revealed that THE SON OF GOD SHOULD DESTROY THE WORKS OF THE DEVIL, AND TAKE THIS RANSOMED WORLD FROM THE USURPER'S GRASP. As they waited in hope, so wait we with all the righteous, knowing it shall shortly be done.

As we look onward to the end, how marvelous the whole career of Satan and his angels! God created him. God exalted him. God tested him. God suffered him. God imprisoned him. God reprieved him. God overthrew him. God punished him forever. Such is the complete outline of revealed demonology. Between every fragment of the inspired history we may write the words:

MYSTERY OF MYSTERIES.

APPENDIX

A GLOSSARY OF DEMONOLOGY

SATAN. In the Old Testament, four times a proper name with the article—Job 1:6, 12; 2:1; Zechariah 3:1. In the Old Testament, without the article—I Chronicles 21:1. As a proper name, thirty-five times in the New Testament.

DEVIL. *Ho Diabolos*. Thirty times in the New Testament.

PRINCE OF THIS WORLD. Four times—John 12:31; 14:30; 16:11; Ephesians 2:2.

WICKED ONE. Six times—Matthew 13:19, 38; I John 2:13, 14; 3:12; 5:18.

TEMPTER. Two times—Matthew 4:3; I Thessalonians 3:5.

DAMONIA. Sixty times in the New Testament. In the plural, forty-one times. Once rendered *gods*—Acts 17:18.

Plural of Devil (*diaboloi*) used three times of human beings—I Tim. 3:11; II Tim. 3:3; Titus 2:3.

127

Cases where Satan or demons are mentioned in the presence of God or His holy messengers. To accuse—Job 1:6. To accuse Ahab—II Chronicles 18:20. To accuse Joshua—Zechariah 3:1, 2. Before Gabriel about Daniel—Daniel 10:13. Before Michael about Moses—Jude 9. Before the Lord Jesus—Matthew 4:1, 8. In the great war of Heaven—Revelation 12:7.

Passages in which *demon* or *evil spirit* should be substituted instead of the word *Devil*, used in the common version:

Matthew 4:24; 7:22; 8:16, 28, 31, 33; 9:32, 33, 34; 10:8; 11:18; 12:22, 24, 27, 28; 15:22; 17:18.

Mark 1:32, 34, 39; 3:15, 22; 5:12, 15, 16, 18; 6:13; 7:26, 29, 30; 9:38; 16:9, 17.

Luke 4:33, 35, 41; 7:33; 8:2, 27, 29, 30, 33, 35, 36, 38; 9:1, 42, 49; 10:17; 11:14, 15, 18, 19, 20; 13:32.

John 8:20; 7:48, 49, 52; 10:20, 21.

I Corinthians 10:20, 21; I Timothy 4:1; James 2:19; 3:15; Revelation 9:20; 16:14; 18:2.